A survival
guide for health
research methods

A survival guide for health research methods

Tracy Ross

Open University Press

Open University Press
McGraw-Hill Education
McGraw-Hill House
Shoppenhangers Road
Maidenhead
Berkshire
England
SL6 2QL

email: enquiries@openup.co.uk
world wide web: www.openup.co.uk

and Two Penn Plaza, New York, NY 10121-2289, USA

First published 2012

Copyright © Tracy Ross 2012

A catalogue record of this book is available from the British Library

ISBN-13: 9780335244737 (pb)
ISBN-10: 0335244734 (pb)
e-ISBN: 9780335244744

Library of Congress Cataloging-in-Publication Data
CIP data has been applied for

Typeset by Aptara Inc., India
Printed in the UK by Bell and Bain Ltd, Glasgow

Fictitious names of companies, products, people, characters and/or data that may be used
herein (in case studies or in examples) are not intended to represent any real individual,
company, product or event.

MIX
Paper from
responsible sources
FSC® C007785

The McGraw·Hill Companies

Praise for this book

"This short book covers all the major issues and perspectives with which health undergraduates must become familiar...It is written in plain English with clear explanations and appropriate examples, along with exercises, articles and glossaries. For those students who approach the topic of research with trepidation, this book will be a welcome and painless introduction."

David Shaw PhD CSci, The Open University, UK

"The author has provided a text that is accessible to a wide range of health students and practitioners...The discussions about how recent is recent evidence is a question that particularly vexes students and this book provides some guidance to the debate, whilst acknowledging there is no easy answer."

Alan Williams, Lecturer, University of Nottingham, UK

Contents

Acknowledgements

I would like to express my thanks to the following people:

Rachel Crookes for her mentorship and guidance.
Marjorie Lloyd for her honest critique.
My husband Ian and daughter Ciara for giving me the space that I needed
to complete this book.

Figures

Tables

Introduction

For any healthcare professional undertaking an academic course of study, research is a fundamental module. As part of the internalization of higher education, research has become as integral to practice as care planning and record keeping. The advent of CHI (Commission For Health Improvement), NICE (National Institute For Clinical Excellence) and Clinical Governance have increased pressure on healthcare practitioners to become more accountable for their actions, hence building research capacity in health care has been recognized as fundamental to evidence based decision making, policy and practice. These organizations stress that quality assured treatment and care must be evidence based while many modern policy documents state that healthcare professionals have a professional and moral responsibility to keep up to date with the developments within their professional practice.

Despite the current demand for evidence based practice, a strong body of evidence confirms that less than 25 per cent of healthcare professionals use research based knowledge in practice (Retsas 2000; Ax and Kincade 2001; Hutchinson and Johnston 2004; Closs and Chester 2006). Thompson (2003) found that most health workers draw on experiential knowledge as the prime source of evidence on which to base their day-to-day clinical decision making, while Thompson et al. (2001) found that many healthcare professionals preferred to use local guidelines, protocols or advice from clinical specialists. Why is this? My own anecdotal experiences as both a healthcare professional and a senior lecturer in research methods have led me to conclude that some healthcare professionals have yet to be convinced of the value of research. Some students have stated that they are 'scared of research as the terminology is complex'; others state that the abundance of studies is 'off-putting' and one student referred to research as being 'trapped in a sweet shop with too much choice and losing your appetite'.

Negative attitudes towards research have also been identified in the literature. It has been suggested that the mere mention of research can induce panic and cognitive freezing. Instead of empowering students and in turn their organizations, this leads to stress and lack of confidence. Stress has been identified as a common component of the student experience but one that has been correlated with poor academic performance, poor coping mechanisms and high attrition rates. It is my view that stress is not useful to students; they need to engage with material in order to understand the content and stress is a barrier to intellectual insight. The implication for practice and learning is that students need increased guidance and coping mechanisms in order to reduce stress and promote understanding. Research is no different to any other course of study; many subjects have complex terminology and jargon entwined within them and could be viewed as 'common sense made hard'. It is quite natural to fear what we do not understand and anecdotal evidence from my students and from students from other universities has revealed that once they are comfortable with the terminology they embrace and enjoy the study of research.

This book is intended to take the stress out of research learning by offering realistic, practical guidance in a learner-friendly way and to provide a real 'survival guide' to any introductory research course. Key concepts, theories and terminology will all be explained clearly, using examples, exercises and reflective opportunities. Each section concludes with a jargon busting component which enables students to identify any complex words or terminology and explore the meaning. This book has the potential to empower students and increase personal, professional and academic confidence in this important area. The book is not intended to guide students through an expansive research project but is intended to increase personal, professional and academic confidence.

Readership

This book is intended as a core text for any healthcare professional undertaking an undergraduate research programme. It will also be useful to any healthcare professional who feels that they lack confidence, knowledge or skill in utilizing research in practice. It will also be of use to staff returning to practice and those with no prior research knowledge. The book's straightforward nature will appeal to international markets and any readers who just wish to explore the research process for personal interest. As every university and healthcare organization values research as a core principle, it is anticipated that there is the potential for wide participation.

Features

This book is simple and reader friendly so that students can engage with the material in a relaxed manner. The multi-method approach considers the variety of readers' learning styles enabling them to grasp theories and concepts according to their own personal needs. Few books direct students on the art of critical writing; this book acknowledges critical reading, thinking and writing as fundamental to confidence and the critical review section in Chapter 10 provides useful tips for surviving and exceeding in a course of study.

Each chapter contains simple aims and objectives in order to signpost the reader and concludes with the opportunity to critically reflect upon the learning accomplished. The simplistic language and short exercises will encourage students to engage with the text in order to promote personal confidence and academic interest. Translating research findings into clinical reality remains a challenge but with a positive attitude and a relaxed learning tool it is achievable.

Background

This book has been developed in response to the writer's experience as an undergraduate research lecturer for eight years and is therefore grounded in reality. Real student stresses and experiences have been reflected upon to produce relevant learning exercises and practical guidance. Qualitative feedback, evaluations and actively listening to students have provided the necessary insight to develop the chapters required for surviving a research course.

References

Ax, S. and Kincade, E. (2001) Nursing students perceptions of research: Usefulness, implementation and training, *Journal of Advanced Nursing*, 31: 599–606.

Closs, S.J. and Chester, F.M. (2006) The effectiveness of methods of dissemination, *Journal of International Medicine*, 21(2): 14–20.

Hutchinson, A.M. and Johnston, L. (2004) Bridging the divide: a survey of nurse's opinions regarding barriers to, and facilitation of, research utilization in the practice setting, *Journal of Clinical Nursing*, 13: 304–15.

Retsas, A. (2000) Barriers to using research evidence in nursing practice, *Journal of Advanced Nursing*. 31: 599–606.

Thompson, C. (2003) What decisions do nurses make? *Journal of Advanced Nursing*, 43: 230–37.

Thompson, C., McCaughan, D., Cullum, N., Sheldon, T.A., Thompson, D.R. and Mullhall, A. (2001) Research information in nurses clinical decision making: What is useful? *Journal of Advanced Nursing*, 36(3): 376–88.

1 Evidence based practice

The unknown is unacceptable; evidence is a human safety net
(Smith et al. 2004)

Introduction

This chapter will explore the meaning of evidence based practice and help to clarify its place in the modern healthcare system. The chapter will explore:

- the rationale for evidence based practice;
- definitions of evidence based practice;
- the nature of knowledge and the relevance of different types of knowledge upon decision making;
- the barriers to research utilization.

Learning outcomes

At the end of this chapter you will be able to:

- critically discuss the rationale for evidence based practice;
- define evidence based practice;
- identify different types of knowledge and reflect upon their relevance;
- effectively define research terms that relate to evidence based practice;
- discuss the barriers to evidence based practice.

Why use evidence based practice?

There are many compelling reasons for adopting an evidence based approach to health care; we will explore some of them in this chapter.

To provide effective care

As a student and healthcare professional the term evidence based practice will probably be very common to you. You do not all need to be researchers and that is not the objective of this book but you need to use research in order to inform practice, ensure safety and monitor effectiveness. You are told constantly to question and justify the actions of yourself and those of others in order to offer patients choices and to provide the most effective care possible. You are expected to give a clear rationale for the healthcare choices that you make and demonstrate an understanding of the evidence for your decisions.

You have a professional responsibility to practice evidence based care in order to empower your individual profession through the use of knowledge but there also exists a moral necessity as healthcare practitioners are accountable to society for the care that they deliver. Sick people are vulnerable and trust those with expert knowledge to advocate on their behalf through the delivery of the best care possible; you can only deliver the best if you know what the best is. In order to determine the best you have to investigate. Healthcare providers have a duty to safeguard all patients from harm and minimize risk. Practising health care in the absence of up to date knowledge is risky and a threat to patient safety. It could be argued that thoughtless care is a form of unintentional abuse as the patient's vulnerability is increased. While the majority of healthcare providers acknowledge the potential effects of physical and emotional harm by careless acts or omissions, many do not adequately consider the harm caused through lack of applied evidence.

To fulfil your role and meet your job criteria

Evidence based practice is now included in job descriptions and gateways to advancement such as *The Knowledge and Skills Framework* (Department of Health 2004) which identifies the key knowledge and skills required for posts and guides individual development. Professional rationales are also dictated through policy and organizational infrastructures. The *Designed For Life* document (Welsh Assembly Government 2005) emphasizes that quality assured treatment and care must be evidence based while the *Modernising Nursing Careers* document (Department of Health 2006) stresses that healthcare professionals have a professional and moral responsibility to keep up to date with the developments within their professional practice.

Exercise 1.1

Obtain a copy of a policy document that relates to your area of professional practice. Does the document discuss evidence based practice? Does it identify evidence based practice as important to your work?

List the advantages of using evidence based practice for:

- patients
- professionals
- organizations

Your list could include some of those given in Table 1.1 but you should be able to expand this list to include your personal thoughts and experiences:

Table 1.1 Advantages of evidence based practice

Patients	Practitioners	Organization
Reduces the amount of time wasted on inappropriate care options	Professional empowerment through enhanced knowledge	Enhance quality of service delivery as practitioners can draw upon a variety of options
Increased consistency as all patients receive the same level of care	Increased personal and professional confidence in problem solving as practitioners adopt a critical approach	Enhanced confidence in the workforce as decision making is reflected in enhanced care outcomes
Increased confidence in practitioners as their knowledge of options is transparent	Increased quality of care through patient satisfaction and positive healthcare outcomes	Reduction in complaints and litigation
Increased value for money	Protection against litigation through rationales for action	Observable commitment to clinical governance
Reduced variation of services	Ability to scientifically support actions	Increased cost effectiveness and value for money
Evidence can be used to support the need for additional resources	Appraise options and interventions	Evidence for the allocation of resources

Up-to-date evidence

Many professional and government documents dictate that care must be up to date and based upon the best available evidence but what does up to date really mean and how do you know what the best evidence is? Many definitions of evidence based practice refer to the term 'up to date' but few authors clarify this term for students. Some academics accept work that is written within ten years while others argue that even work written within five years can be out of date. The term 'up-to-date evidence' indicates that the most recent evidence is the best but this should not necessarily be accepted as no study is perfect. Every piece of evidence should be evaluated for its strengths and weaknesses.

Example
Imagine that you have two research papers. Paper 1 was published in 2009, and states that children run faster following the ingestion of chocolate. To test this statement 10 children from a school in London were given a bar of chocolate prior to running in a 100 metre race. The results showed that 7/10 children who were given chocolate performed faster than the children who did not receive chocolate prior to their races.

Paper 2 was published in 2002 and also stated that chocolate aids running. In this study chocolate was administered to 2,234 children from 10 counties within the United Kingdom. However, only 29 of the children given chocolate won their races.

Consider which of these two papers you would rather believe and why.

Despite the fact that paper 1 is more current, it is less credible due to the very small group of 10 children compared to a group of 2,234 children in paper 2. Paper 1 only focused on a small number of children in one city, whereas paper 2 used more children from many areas and is more likely to reflect the reality of children the UK and may be considered more believable. This is not a comprehensive example of how to appraise evidence as this is covered in detail in Chapter 10 but it demonstrates that 'current' is not necessarily 'best' evidence. This example highlights that all studies, regardless of their currency, should be competently appraised in order to have value. However, this still fails to adequately define good evidence.

Defining best evidence

One of the earliest and most commonly used definitions of evidence based practice is provided by Sackett et al. (1996: 71): evidence based practice is

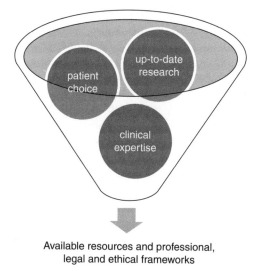

Available resources and professional,
legal and ethical frameworks

Figure 1.1 Evidence based practice.

'the conscientious, explicit and judicious use of current best evidence in making decisions'. Although this was originally a medical definition, it has relevance to other professions as put simply, Sackett is saying that good decision making is about using evidence carefully (with deep thought and critique), sensibly (it should be necessary) and clearly (it should be easy to understand).

Neale (2009: 8) adds that evidence based practice 'is underpinned by the belief that practitioners should make rational decisions on the basis of structured critical appraisals of empirical evidence relating to what works in their field'. What do these definitions mean to you, are they easy definitions to understand? Is anything missing?

One of the simplest definitions of evidence based practice is provided by Pape (2003: 155): evidence based practice is the 'combination of the best research evidence, clinical experience and clients desires'. Pape's definition can be summarized as in Figure 1.1. The simplicity of Pape's definition is admirable as it considers clinical expertise and patient preference. However, this relies upon the healthcare professional knowing the patient and understanding their cultural patterns. This involves spending time and developing deep dialogue with the patient. Morse (1994) refers to this process as using your knowledge as a human in order to read the patient. While this is a preferred mode of practice, it may be criticized as idealistic as, although you are expected to use empathy in practice, the extent to which you can ever really understand another person's reality is highly questionable. Although this definition acknowledges the perspectives of three major stakeholders, it is unclear which type of evidence prevails in the event of conflict. Furthermore, the definition fails to consider organizational and financial constraints such as the distribution of resources and power structures that impinge upon personal choice. There may be current, valid and reliable evidence available that is agreeable to the patient and practitioner but if the resources are not available to purchase the care, it will not be an outcome. Hence, this definition still fails to adequately define what best evidence is.

Example
A common example of conflicting perspectives could be where a patient requests antibiotic therapy but evidence shows that antibiotics increase resistance and have little benefit for patients. Health professionals may believe in the evidence against prescribing antibiotics but the patient may not and may rely upon their personal or experiential knowledge. If a good evidence based decision considers all of the stakeholders, what happens to that decision in the event of conflict?

Sackett tried to clarify some of the terms used to define evidence in a later definition:

> Evidence based care is the integration of clinical expertise, patient values, and the best evidence into the decision making process for patient care. Clinical expertise refers to the clinician's cumulated experience, education and clinical skills. The patient brings to the encounter his or her own personal and unique concerns, expectations, and values. The best evidence is usually found in clinically relevant research that has been conducted using sound methodology. (Sackett 2002: 1)

Here Sackett acknowledges and values the different types of knowledge held by the clinician, for example, knowledge acquired through cultural and personal experiences, logical and critical knowledge gained through curriculum and the extra insight that can only be acquired through cumulative clinical expertise. He values the patient as an empowered decision maker and highlights that not all research is transferable into practice due to flaws in either design or reason.

Exercise 1.2

Based on the discussion so far, can you identify the main components of evidence based decision making? Some suggestions are made in the Appendix.

This section has attempted to define some of the characteristics of evidence based practice but has not clarified the nature of evidence itself. In order to enhance understanding it is sometimes easier to illustrate what something is not rather than to try and describe what it may be, therefore we will explore types of knowledge and evaluate their relevance to decision making.

Types of knowledge

The term 'evidence based' implies some scientific contribution and rationality, however Aveyard and Sharp (2009) advocate that different types of decision making need different types of evidence. Some types of evidence are sufficient to guide us through everyday life but fail to offer the desired level of clinical direction needed for professional practice. Hence health professionals tend to adopt an eclectic approach to decision making, drawing on knowledge from several areas. This section will discuss five sources of knowledge that may be used to guide decision making (see Figure 1.2). Each of these will be critically related to evidence based decision making in this chapter.

Traditional knowledge

Traditional or indigenous knowledge refers to the longstanding, passed down wisdom that occurs between communities. It could be described as knowledge

Figure 1.2 Types of knowledge.

gained by living next to nature that distinguishes one community from another. It may be termed socially constructed knowledge as it is deeply embedded in cultural life patterns and inextricably bound in rituals and religious practices. Much of the knowledge is gained through revelation, for example in stories, songs or pictures. Although some critics refer to indigenous knowledge as unscientific and tacit, it has an inherent rationality and it has its uses in terms of practical commonsense survival within a particular culture. For example, understanding the rituals, beliefs and religions of local people allows predictions to be made about needs within local areas and may be crucial to social workers, health visitors or police. Some examples of these follow:

- If a particular local area has a high percentage of devoted Muslims who need to pray at particular times, knowledge of these times would be useful to health visitors so that visits could be planned in order to preserve respect.
- If a particular local area has a high population of practising Catholic people, this could have an impact upon the type of sexual health education that is offered. For example rather than focusing on issuing contraception, the healthcare professional may focus upon safe sexual practices.
- If a particular group have strong beliefs about the preservation of animals, healthcare services may focus upon how to obtain a healthy state through optimizing minerals and vegetables.

The extent to which this form of evidence may be termed reliable is questionable as it is difficult to generalize knowledge between cultures, however its strength lies in its validity. As much of the knowledge is sacred it is accepted as truth for the people concerned. Understanding tradition and culture is crucial to understanding the organization that you work in as many work patterns are rooted in rituals, for example: meal times, patient handovers, the organization of shift patterns. Most importantly traditional knowledge is fundamental to promoting caring, dignity and respect. Understanding a patient's cultural norms has the potential to reduce anxiety, aid holistic assessment and considerately plan culturally relevant interventions.

Authority knowledge

Authority or autocratic knowledge is carried down from experts to novices and is evident in every society; examples include: parent–child, teacher–student, employer–employee relationships. This form of evidence is also socially constructed and plays a role in maintaining social order. However, it is the most short-lasting form of evidence as it relies upon the reputation and expertise of the knowledge giver. As the knowledge receiver gains more knowledge or the social situation changes, the knowledge giver becomes less credible. Authority knowledge is dependent upon the group members believing and respecting both the knowledge giver and the knowledge itself. Group members are less likely to comply with the outcomes of this knowledge as they lack ownership. Authority knowledge is used to inform decision making in health care through the prescribing of medication or referral to additional services such as physiotherapy.

Personal knowledge

Personal or experiential knowledge is knowledge that is gained through experience throughout life, for example, experiencing a fall or an accident. Due to its subjectivity anecdotal or personal evidence is considered less reliable and robust than any other form of evidence. While tradition and authority evidence have some internal logic and have some level of transferability, personal evidence is considered too person centred to generalize to another human being. It is deemed impossible to audit the trail of knowledge as one cannot enter the brain of another human being. In many published hierarchies of evidence such as University of York NHS Centre for Reviews and Dissemination, personal knowledge is not even acknowledged. However, much of the health professional's work involves empathy and understanding the humanity of others. This cannot be achieved without some level of introspection and self-awareness, therefore the experiences that a person is exposed to will impact the way in which they perceive events and react to them. For example, Benner and Wrubel (1989) claims that caring has to be experienced in order to be recognized as caring and without this experience a person cannot know how to model caring acts.

If the subject of ethics is used as an example of personal knowledge, in order to recognize the human rights of others, one has to identify with self in order to recognize and categorize a right. However, for the individual making the clinical decision this is the most powerful and most trustworthy source of evidence as it has been personally validated. Carper (1978) acknowledges that personal knowledge is crucial to clinical expertise and includes it in her 'Four fundamental patterns of knowing'. An example where personal knowledge is used to inform decision making could include female healthcare professionals who have experienced childbirth being able to predict when a new mother may need analgesia or being able to offer useful tips about breastfeeding. However, it must be noted that personal experience lacks the reliability of research based evidence and should not be used alone to guide healthcare practices. Personal knowledge can be an aid to caring through the sharing of experiences and promotion of empathy but can lead to biased professional judgements.

Trial and error knowledge

The trial and error approach involves the successive use of alternatives until some level of success is achieved and is often used in the absence of more concrete knowledge. It involves systematically trying new strategies, rejecting those that are flawed and accepting those that work. It may be termed solution orientated and problem specific as it is very focused in its approach to discovery. Hence, one could argue that there are some scientific principles involved and it could be likened to the formulation and testing of strategies in experiments and randomized control trials (Parahoo 2006). This approach is used in the selection of wound care dressings or drug therapies. As patients are individuals, different therapies will work for different people; sometimes healthcare professionals have to try a variety of approaches from the resources that are available until one is successful. This type of evidence has the potential to produce innovation but is high risk and clinicians often fail to analyse the reasons for failure or scrutinize the reason for success.

Research based knowledge

Research based evidence is evidence produced from scientific studies. Research is highly regarded by healthcare professionals as it uses systematic methods to solve complex social problems by drawing on statistics. However, research based evidence also draws upon the many other forms of knowledge, for example, successful interviewing requires some understanding of traditional behaviour while randomized control trials involve an element of trial and error. For example, a randomized control trial involves researchers testing one or more interventions on groups of people without any concrete knowledge of the outcomes. Research has its value in establishing cause and effect, providing evidence for measuring the effectiveness of interventions and understanding the nature of experiences and therefore deserves its place in any discussion of evidence based practice. Research informs decision making by evaluating which interventions work better than others so that patients receive the most effective care strategy. Hamer and Collinson (2005) argue that research based evidence can enhance clinical judgement through the critical application of reliable and valid data but cannot and should not replace it.

Parahoo (2006) describes research as a systematic way of knowing that lays bare its methods for all to see. This implies that research is honest and transparent and therefore should be reliable and trustworthy. However, Parahoo goes on to argue that research is dependent upon the quality of the research design itself. Smith et al. (2004) add that additional functions include securing professional status, protection from litigation and to evaluate the use of resources. They go on to argue that not all health work is amenable to scientific investigation; for example, Watson (2004) argues that the concept of caring cannot be measured as it cannot be adequately defined. An example of research based knowledge would be Livesley's (2005) study into how children's nurses interpret work with unaccompanied hospitalized children in Manchester. Livesley used tape-recorded interviews with four children's nurses in order to explore the strategies that nurses use to meet the needs of children who are unaccompanied by their parents while in hospital. The study found that nurses used distancing to create professional boundaries and as a way of distinguishing between the parent and nurse roles.

Exercise 1.3

Consider the five types of knowledge that have been discussed. Which do you perceive as the most relevant to your profession? Think of incidents from your practice where you have used each type of knowledge and reflect upon the outcome of your decision making.

- traditional knowledge
- authority knowledge
- personal knowledge
- trial and error knowledge
- research based knowledge

Barriers to using evidence based practice

While many authors support the use of evidence based practice, less attention has been paid to developing comfort with the term and understanding the nature of evidence and what it means for you on a day-to-day basis. Much of the literature that discusses evidence based practice is woolly and jargon laden. Meanings are often inferred rather than made clear. Glaziou and Haynes (2005) suggest that this results in underuse and misuse of evidence. They claim that research that should change practice is underused due to lack of: understanding, time, power to introduce change and skills in critical appraisal.

Example
Imagine that you are preparing to write an essay for your research course. While collecting material for your essay, you come across several pieces of research that could be used to inform practice. The articles suggest new ways to perform an activity within your working area. You take these to your

manager/mentor who states that he/she is too busy to make changes at the moment; furthermore, the rest of the staff state that they like things the way they are. Although the research may be 'out there' you may not be able to implement it.

Research is over used when handed down anecdotally by experts or specialist healthcare professionals. It is often quicker to ask a considered expert than to personally explore the literature. This results in staff knowing the right thing to do but not knowing why it is the right thing.

Example

How many times do you hear staff use the term 'research states that we should do this' but when you ask 'which research?' the answer is not forthcoming?

Research is misused due to the abundance of studies with competing claims and advice. Glaziou and Haynes (2005) point out that Medline alone indexes more than 560 000 new articles per year and there is often little effort to set the results systematically in the context of similar studies. This limits the usefulness of research at the bedside as staff members lose trust in the findings and evidence is not transformed into action. To commit to evidence based practice clinicians need effective strategies for extracting relevant information from the many publications currently available. Materials need to be current, accessible and user friendly. To ease the burden of information overload and make the system more user friendly, several services exist to help practitioners tap into just those articles relevant to their specific area of practice. Examples include: *Evidence-Based Nursing* (Journal), The Cochrane Library and bmjupdates. Each of these offer valid and reliable overviews of studies that can save students valuable time and expense.

The challenge of implementing change can itself be a disincentive to applying research into practice as changing behaviour is complex and clinicians will often revert back to usual practices unless they genuinely believe in the evidence for change. The abundance of conflicting research based evidence impacts people's confidence in the findings and deters them from implementing new strategies as the strategies are perceived as too high risk.

Exercise 1.4

Identify the factors that would/could deter you from implementing evidence in your area of practice. (Examples are provided in the Appendix.) Can you think of any strategies to reduce the barriers that you have identified?

Summary

This chapter has explored the place of evidence based practice in the modern healthcare system. The rationality for using different types of evidence has been critically discussed and the value of eclectic decision making has been established if we want to create wise clinicians. Effective decision making could be defined as the synthesis of science and sensibility through the use of research, tradition, experiences, experimentation and direction from authority. Different events call for different types of knowledge. This chapter has highlighted the strengths and weaknesses of five types of knowledge as they relate to health care. Begley (2009) points out that wisdom is the appropriate use of knowledge and goes on to stress that the practitioner who lacks the wisdom to use knowledge well will practise poorly. Evidence based practice is a craft and like most crafts, it needs engagement, nurture and refinement.

Reflective activity

Consider the following opposing statements about evidence based practice. Which one do you believe and why?

1   Evidence based practice is the mindless application of population studies in order to predict treatment for the individual. It takes the results of studies of large groups of people and tries to apply them to individuals who may have unique circumstances or characteristics, not found in the study groups. Therefore, research is not necessarily useful.
2   'Evidence based practice converts the abstract exercise of reading and appraising the literature into the useful process of using the literature to benefit individual patients while simultaneously expanding the clinician's knowledge base' Bordley (1997: 427).

Reflecting upon these statements may encourage you to consider your viewpoint and commitment to evidence based practice. To what extent do you practise evidence based practice? Are there any barriers to implementing evidence that you can now address?

Jargon busting

Make a list of any words in this chapter that you do not understand. Look up their meaning and think about how the words relate to research and health care. You may like to consider some of these:

Appraise: To critically evaluate the worth of something. Often used to compare and contrast different pieces of research or individual research papers.

Conscientious: Very carefully, with thought and deliberation. This is often used to imply that evidence should be thoroughly thought through before being acted upon.

Empowerment: Enabling people to feel that they have the power and freedom to make decisions. This can be used when considering ethical issues in research.

Evidence: Gathering information in order to make a decision or form some understanding about something. Can be used to guide healthcare activities, change patterns of thinking or justify behaviours.

Experiential knowledge: Knowledge that has been gained from living out particular situations. It can be used to describe experiences in some types of research.

Explicit: Open and unambiguous. This is used to imply that research should be clear and not have any misleading information.

Infrastructures: The component parts that make up organizations such as healthcare institutions. It can refer to rules, laws, power structures, facilities or equipment.

Judicious: Sensible and wise. This is used to imply that research should be used cautiously to do good and not just because it exists.

Randomized control trial: A form of experiment where two groups are used to test a theory. One group is a control group (who would not be given a drug for example) and one group are an experimental group (for example, this group would receive a given drug). Every person in the study group has an equal chance of selection into one of the two groups.

Robust: Strong. Used to evaluate how good a piece of research is. The term implies that the research has been carried out with minimal flaws or mistakes.

Stakeholder: This refers to all of the people involved in a given situation who may hold a viewpoint. This can be used when considering ethical issues in research.

References

Aveyard, H. and Sharp, P. (2009) *A Beginners Guide to Evidence Based Practice in Health and Social Care*. Maidenhead: McGraw-Hill.

Begley, J. (2009) Readers response, *Evidence Based Midwifery*, 17(3): 3.

Benner, P. and Wrubel, J. (1989) *The Primacy of Caring: Stress and Coping in Health and Illness*. Menlo Park, CA: Addison-Wesley.

Bordley, D.R. (1997) Evidence-based medicine: a powerful educational tool for clerkship education, *American Journal of Medicine*, 102(5): 427–32.

Carper, B. (1978) Fundamental patterns of knowing, *Advances in Nursing Science*, 1(1): 13–23.

Department of Health (2004) *The Knowledge and Skills Framework*. London: Department of Health.

Department of Health (2006) *Modernising Nursing Careers*. London: Department of Health.

Glaziou, P. and Haynes, B. (2005) The paths from research to improved health care, *Evidence-Based Nursing*, 8: 36–8.

Hamer, S. and Collinson, G. (2005) *Achieving Evidence-based Practice: A Handbook for Practitioners*. London: Baillier Tindall.

Livesley, J. (2005) Telling tales: a qualitative exploration of how children's nurses interpret work with unaccompanied hospitalised children, *Journal of Clinical Nursing*, 14(1): 43.

Morse, J.M. (1994) *Critical Issues in Qualitative Research Methodology*. London: Sage.

Neale, J. (2009) *Research Methods for Health and Social Care*. Basingstoke: Palgrave Macmillan.

Pape, T.M. (2003) Evidence based nursing practice. To infinity and beyond, *The Journal of Continuing Education in Nursing*, 34: 154–61.

Parahoo, K. (2006) *Nursing Research, Principles, Process and Issues*, 2nd edn. Basingstoke: Palgrave Macmillan.

Sackett, D.L., Rosenburg, W.M.C., Muir Gray, J.A., Haynes, R.B. and Richardson, W.S. (1996) Evidence-based Medicine, what it is and what it isn't, *British Medical Journal*, 312: 71–2.

Sackett, D. (2002) *Evidence-based Medicine: How to Practise and Teach EBM*, 2nd edn. London: Churchill Livingstone.

Smith, P., James, T., Lorentzon, M. and Pope, R. (2004) *Evidence Based Nursing and Health Care*. London: Churchill Livingstone.

Watson, J. (2004) *Caring Science as Sacred Science*. Philadelphia, CA: F.A. Davis.

Welsh Assembly Government (2005) *Designed For Life*. Cardiff: WAG.

2 The nature of research

Introduction

We use research in our everyday lives to guide our decisions and actions. For example, when purchasing food we investigate the options available, compare and contrast their features, think about the findings and what they mean, and then make an informed decision about which foods to purchase and which to reject. The same process can be applied when booking a holiday or buying a car. Put simply, we apply a systematic process to gain more knowledge about the world around us. Research is a finding out activity, so what distinguishes research from other types of finding out activities? 'Research is a language game. Like any game, a language game is subject to a series of rules; knowing the rules allows one to participate' (Carson and Fairbairn 2002).

Burns and Grove (2005) refer to research as entering a new world while Carson and Fairbairn refer to it as a game. It may be viewed as both as entering any new world requires mastery of a new language, learning and applying new rules and norms and infiltrating the culture in order to interact effectively. Understanding research terminology and culture will allow you to play the research game. The aim of this chapter is to clarify the nature of research and identify the core elements that inform the research process. This chapter differentiates research from non-research and provides an introduction to the two dominant research paradigms.

Learning outcomes

At the end of this chapter you will be able to:

- define the term research;
- identify the key features of research;
- differentiate between research and non-research;
- describe the research process.

What is research?

Succinct, all-encompassing definitions of research are sparse; Cormack (2000) attributes this to the assumption that the meaning of research is self-evident and needs no clarification. This assumes that there exists one entity called research and that this research can be easily defined and understood. Historically, medicine has held the monopoly in research which has created definitions rooted in empirics, science and objectivity. Lacey (1999) points out that health professionals allied to medicine are still relative newcomers to research culture and lack their own body of research knowledge and therefore still subscribe to existing knowledge from medicine, philosophy and the social sciences. This puts them in a weaker position when it comes to validating new knowledge. However, she points out that this does not deter healthcare professionals from manipulating and refining established practices to fit their purpose and attempting to create a new eclectic body of research knowledge.

Research has been perceived as an elitist, academic endeavour performed by those at the pinnacle of their careers, a medical activity or one performed by drug companies in laboratories. Lacey identified that despite the drive towards evidence based practice, many healthcare professionals are still afraid of research and do not understand the terminology. Her study concluded that several participants could summon up appropriate research terms but they could not actually define the term research when asked.

Research has been defined as the search for knowledge through systematic enquiry (Macleod Clark and Hockey (1989), a harnessing of curiosity (Waters 2009) and a culture (Mulhall and Le May 1999). These definitions imply that research is a form of critical thinking that is motivated by internal, value-laden agendas. Robson (2002) asserts that there are three key features that distinguish research from other finding out activities:

- It is about sceptical thinking and critically reviewing existing knowledge.
- It is concerned with following a specific systematic process.
- It has ethical implications.

Exercise 2.1

Consider the process that you would use to book a holiday. Describe the method and place the steps into an ordered form. Would you consider this to be research? Identify any similarities and differences between research and booking a holiday.

Does booking a holiday involve the three key features identified by Robson? Again ask yourself the question, is this a form of research? *Why/why not?*

The word research originally derives from the French 'recherché' which means to search closely. This implies that research is concerned with investigation, method and thinking. The term search also implies that there is a practical aspect to research: it is more than just theorizing and concluding, it is physical work. Therefore it may be regarded as an activity motivated by an inquisitiveness to gain some new insight into a problem, issue or just to understand the world around us.

The Frascati Manual (1993:4) summed up research as: 'creative work undertaken on a systematic basis in order to increase the stock of knowledge, including knowledge of man, culture and society and the use of this stock of knowledge to devise new applications'. Sridhar (2010:1) goes further to add that research is: 'The process of arriving at dependable solutions to problems through the planned and systematic collection, analysis and interpretation of data'. He adds that research should be objective, reproducible, relevant and capable of having some control over the factors under investigation. This implies that research has built-in mechanisms that protect against error, bias, subjectivity and harm.

So, research is about:

- thinking
- planning
- action
- ethics
- control
- change

Research is a term that describes a process of enquiry that has at its heart a systematic approach, a theoretical foundation and a purposeful intention. This implies a voyage of discovery with the potential for innovation and the discovery of new worlds. However, it is important to acknowledge that not all healthcare research is concerned with transforming practice; sometimes the objective is to seek a deeper understanding of experiences or to confirm or refute what may already be known.

There are several ways to categorize research; for example, it can be separated into pure or applied.

Pure research

> Neither god, science, reason, philosophy or poetry can satisfy our longing for the stability to guide our thoughts and actions. (Bernstein 1983).

This quote from Bernstein implies that humans are curious animals who are constantly seeking out new information even if the data is not immediately relevant. It also implies that we constantly seek explanations for our actions. It is this basic curiosity that justifies the place of pure research. Pure research (sometimes referred to as basic research, fundamental research or romantic research) arises out of curiosity about the world around us and may have no direct health or commercial benefits. It focuses on explaining, exploring or describing how and why the world operates in particular ways. It focuses on supporting or refuting theories about social relationships and world events which in turn lead to the generation of new ideas, principles and theories. Its aim is to nourish the expansion of new knowledge and advance knowledge for its own sake, providing new insights into human behaviour.

Example
Consider the issue of pain. There are many studies that explore patients' perceptions of pain; most of these identify physical, psychological, social and spiritual aspects. Knowing these dimensions helps us to recognize and empathize with people's pain but does not actually change the nature of the pain or enable us to care any differently. However, this information is crucial to understanding how humans work and why they may react in certain ways to stimuli. Here, pure research has led to understanding but not created any change.

Although pure research has no intention to create change, it is often the foundation for new practice and provides the basis for applied research and modern progress. For example Watson (1979) set out to define the meaning of caring in order to enhance understanding of the term. Her work has been used as a foundation for many other researchers who have tried to devise models of caring that can be used to: raise consciousness of caring (Benner and Wrubel 1989), define caring behaviours (Morrison and Burnard 1997) and teach caring through education (Ross 2000).

Applied research

Unlike pure research applied research provides a direct link between theory and practice in that it has a specific problem to solve or investigate. Applied research advances practice and creates innovation through the application of theory and resolutions. It can provide the rationale and direction for change and is purposeful rather than romantic. For example, applied research can be used to collect data about healing rates in wounds, identify how demographics impact disease rates, which drugs act on which receptors sites, which products consumers prefer and many other problem-related areas. Tatum (2003) claims that every organizational entity uses applied research as, by their nature, every organization has problems to solve. He refers to applied research as: 'Any fact gathering project that is conducted with an eye to acquiring and applying knowledge that will address a specific problem or meet a specific need . . . . leading to new and improved offerings' (p. 23).

Tatum is claiming that there are two distinct elements to applied research: research and development. There is an investigative function and a strategy developing function. For example, Orpen and Harris's (2010) study is an example of research with an investigative function and a developmental function as it led to direct change. The researchers carried out a qualitative study to explore patient's perceptions of preoperative home-based occupational therapy services. The findings of the study confirmed the worth of home-based preoperative occupational services but it highlighted that physiotherapy services were less useful in the preoperative stage. This study was then used by the NHS trust to design future service delivery that resulted in the withdrawal of physiotherapy services in the preoperative stage.

Tatum points out that neither investigation or strategy development are without complexities as in the modern cost conscious NHS, research must be seen as delivering measurable results in terms of improved patient care; she adds that research that gains credit for the researcher but then 'sits on a shelf' is of no use and may not be worth the investment. The assumption is made that the research produced through the applied research method will lead to positive strategies and outcomes; however, research is only as robust as the researcher and the methods employed and not all problems can be solved by research. Parahoo (2006) adds that research findings by themselves are not solutions to problems; they may provide new insight but decisions should still utilize other forms of knowledge before being implemented. For example, the culture and political ideals of the organization may impact which research is adopted or perhaps the resources available may impact the chosen strategy. However, Tatum points out that regardless of the outcome, applied research enhances the public profile of the organization and improves the opportunities for meeting the institutional goals.

Exercise 2.2

Think about both styles of research discussed above. What do you think are the advantages and disadvantages of each type of research? Some suggestions are made in Figure 2.1 in order to enhance your understanding.

Research is not one singular process; it has multiple designs and methods to achieve its aims. The approach chosen will depend upon the question that needs to be answered. Bowling (2009) acknowledges that there is no hierarchy of excellence with regards to methods and designs as different approaches are appropriate for different types of enquiry. For example Borbasi et al. (2004)

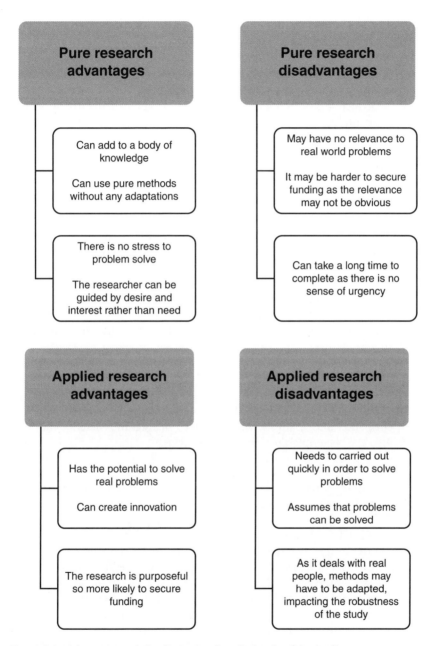

Figure 2.1 Advantages and disadvantages of applied and pure research.

claim that research adopts two types of knowledge according to the question that needs to be answered:

- Inductive reasoning allows us to generate new knowledge and theories.
- Deductive reasoning allows us to test out existing theories and reasoning.

Induction and deduction

Deduction tends to be viewed as the scientific approach to research in that the researcher starts with an idea, develops a theory and then tests the theory by applying scientific principles and approaches such as experiments or surveys. After formulating a theory, the researcher reviews the existing literature in order to generate a question or statement that can be tested; this is referred to as the 'hypothesis'. This approach builds upon previous research in order to understand why certain things occur and what their causes are. However, this assumes that a body of knowledge is already in existence. Sometimes knowledge about a specific topic does not exist and this is where inductive knowledge is useful.

Inductive knowledge begins with ideas or observations and builds them into either acceptable theories or testable hypotheses. Induction is often viewed as the preliminary stage where theory is produced and then tested deductively later. So we can see that induction starts with small pieces of knowledge and builds it into a whole, rather like a jigsaw whereas deduction starts with the bigger picture and breaks it down.

Example
An easy way to differentiate between inductive and deductive approaches could be to consider how detectives investigate a murder. Some detectives use a deductive approach to solving a crime in that they have theory about who committed the murder at the start of the investigation and accumulate clues to prove or disprove the theory. An example of this would be if we were to watch the American TV detective series *Columbo*. This show identifies the murderer at the start of the show and goes on to demonstrate how Columbo theorizes about the identity of the murderer and shows how he reaches his conclusions. In contrast, some detectives have no prior assumptions as to the murderer's identity and collect clues in order to formulate a theory at the end. This would be an example of an inductive approach and is practised by the TV detective Poirot who reveals the murderer's identity at the end of the show once all the available clues have been gathered and analysed. The two types of research knowledge could be summarized as in Figure 2.2.

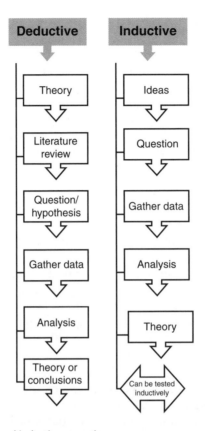

Figure 2.2   Deductive and inductive reasoning.

Both induction and deduction have their place in research and the stages that are used within each style directs the research process. There are two types of research called quantitative and qualitative; these will be discussed in depth in the next chapters. Quantitative research uses deduction as it starts with a theory and attempts to prove it while qualitative research uses an inductive approach as it asks a question but produces a theory at the end of the study.

****

To summarize the discussion so far, research has been defined as a process of enquiry that involves sceptical thought, has a specific systematic approach, involves physical work and has ethical considerations. It involves theory generating and theory testing and may be carried out to satisfy academic curiosity or applied to real problems. It is an approach to 'finding out' that utilizes multiple types of knowledge such as clinical, personal, cultural, scientific, trial and error and can be validated against existing knowledge. It is different to non-research in that it has built-in mechanisms to protect against error, bias and ethical injury. So, we now have some idea what constitutes research but confusion still exists about what is research and what constitutes other forms of enquiry such as audit, service evaluation, literature review, systematic reviews and meta-analysis. The next section will explore these types of enquiry.

Non-research

Literature review

A literature review is not research, it is a critical exploration of the literature around a given topic. It can be used independently as part of an undergraduate assessment in the form of a dissertation or can be used as part of a research study. It will inform the research, provide direction, put what is already known into context and identify gaps that a study could address. The literature review has many functions that include:

- **justifying the relevance of research topic**: for example McVicar (2003) wanted to highlight how stressed nurses are in the workplace and performed a literature review that explored policy documents and studies over an 18 year period. The literature review demonstrated the importance of organizations understanding the implications of stress for the workforce and highlighted that the initiatives put in place did not offer long-term solutions.
- **preventing the duplication of research**: most research is funded either by research councils, pharmaceutical companies or employing organizations, therefore duplicating research unnecessarily is both labour intensive and expensive. A literature review can communicate issues that need exploring and identify redundant topics.
- **providing benchmarks against which problem solving can be set**: the literature review carried out by McVicar identified the past and current causes of stress in the workplace which could motivate organizations to focus their stress management interventions more realistically.
- **suggesting indicators for changing practice**: the literature review by McVicar identified a clear need for preventative strategies rather than short-term post-stress interventions.

- **allowing concepts to be clarified and explored**: McVicar's literature review explored literature from the United Kingdom, United States of America, New Zealand and Australia and found that the concept of stress was universal but the stressors that caused the stress were interpreted differently in different areas.

What is a literature review?

A literature review involves appraising the strengths and weaknesses of literature, synthesizing and analysing the arguments in order to generate new research questions. This type of review would usually be perfomed as part of the assessment for undergraduate students in their final year of study and enables the student to explore a particular topic of interest in more depth than a normal essay would allow. A literature review may contain some of the features of research in that it is a systematic process of enquiry and therefore critical thought processes are employed during the search for literature and when interacting with the literature. It could be argued that this gives the literature review a scientific quality and scholarly standing; however, the quality of the review is dependent upon the nature of the literature being reviewed, the analytical skills of the writer and the relevance of the findings.

As the number of published studies is rapidly increasing due to the advent of evidence based practice, literature reviews are an ideal time-saving resource for healthcare professionals as instead of searching through the vast amount of data one should be able to just access someone else's review. However, the reality is that most literature reviews remain an academic exercise and are rarely published. Some libraries display students' literature reviews but the quality and standard need to be considered with care. Mulrow et al. (1997) expressed concern about the quality of literature reviews that are published and examined 50 literature reviews from highly reputable medical journals and found that 49 of them had quality issues relating to the standard of the methods and the standard of the summaries.

A literature review is not concerned with anecdotal opinions but draws upon a variety of credible evidence. Electronically accessed journal articles are favoured as these offer concise, up-to-date studies that are usually refereed. The term 'refereed' is used to describe work that has been rigorously reviewed for its reliability and validity by experts prior to publication and is therefore considered more robust that non-refereed work. Although non-refereed work such as that found in trade journals or magazines is less robust, it may still be considered scholarly according to its relevance and currency.

Primary rather than secondary sources should always be used where possible. Research published within five years is considered more credible than older studies; however, some literature may be deemed weak if classic work is not included as this adds context to the study. Conference proceedings and dissertations can also be credible sources of material as they often provide the most up-to-date data. Government reports and books tend to be less up to date as they take longer to write, hence the work can date quicker. They may also adopt a particular stance or ideology which can bias the work; however, they are a useful resource for background material and can provide a good starting point for the topic.

Newspapers and anecdotal articles are considered too biased and general to be of scholarly significance but can provide the catalyst for ideas that can be explored in more credible articles. The internet must be viewed with some caution as articles are rarely expertly reviewed prior to posting and their quality and accuracy may not be relied upon.

Systematic review

Some confusion exists in the literature concerning definitions of literature reviews and systematic reviews. It is argued that a literature review should follow a systematic approach which leads people to use the two terms interchangeably when there are quite distinct differences. A systematic review is considered to be more robust than a literature review in that it adopts a more systematic and structured approach to literature searching. For this reason it is most commonly used to justify resource allocation and interventions used in large organizations. It is considered to be the best source of information for making clinical decisions and ensures that only the best value interventions are adopted. Whereas a literature review may draw upon literature from a variety of different sources, and may be considered 'broad' a systematic review only utilizes research studies in order to answer a specific question and is more focused and narrow in its approach. For example, in Victor's (2009) systematic review only research that explored carers was used whereas Lewis et al. (2009) selected literature that involved the views of healthcare professionals and patients. A systematic review usually aims to answer a specific question in the same way that a research study would. Some systematic reviews contain a hypothesis which the literature will support or reject.

A systematic review relies upon the use of strict inclusion and exclusion criteria in order to ensure the robustness of the work. For example, a narrow time frame may be selected if a mass of literature exists or perhaps only particular types of studies may be included. For instance, it may be that only randomized control trials are relevant or only case studies. As most healthcare professionals are limited in their time and resources, selecting the use of strict criteria frees them from reviewing the potentially large number of studies that may be available.

A good systematic review examines all of the relevant literature about a topic whether it has been published or not; some journals have a particular bias towards types of articles and those that do not meet the criteria may not be published but may be robust and relevant. Excluding any studies can result in a biased review so researchers have to be very clear why some data is included and excluded. Lewis et al. (2009) reviewed only 19 studies in their exploration of patients' and healthcare professionals' views of cancer care follow up whereas Victor (2009) reviewed 107 studies when she investigated the interventions for carers in the UK. Unlike a literature review that is performed by one researcher, two reviewers are usually involved in the process of systematic reviewing which can enhance the reliability of the work as each reviewer gives their opinions independently of each other and then the results are compared for their consistency. Only primary research is acceptable in a systematic review as secondary sources can sometimes contain biases that may influence the findings of the review.

Once the eligible studies have been decided upon the researchers construct a table that clearly identifies the characteristics of the studies and these studies are then assessed for their quality according to predefined criteria. The studies are graded according to high, medium or low quality. The results of the review can be summarized in narrative format such as in a report as in Victor's (2009) systematic review or summarized statistically in the form of a table as in Lewis et al.'s systematic review.

Although systematic reviews are sometimes referred to as 'research on research', they do not fulfil the criteria to be labelled true research as they do not require ethical clearance and do not generate new theory and use databases rather than samples of people for their data. The Cochrane Library, The Centre for Research and Dissemination based in York and National Institute of Clinical Excellence (NICE) remain the key sources of systematic reviews for health care. Systematic reviews are a quick route to establishing the credibility of particular treatment options. The advantage of a systematic review is the time saved for the healthcare professional in terms of searching for and reviewing literature as someone has already done it for them.

Exercise 2.3

Make a list of the differences between a literature review and a systematic review. The answers are provided in the Appendix.

Meta-analysis

A meta-analysis may be viewed as a type of systematic review in that it follows a similar process in the approach to searching and synthesizing studies; however, a meta-analysis goes a stage further in that it statistically analyses the results from all of the available evidence in order to increase the strength of the findings. Statistical pooling and synthesis allows differing features between datasets to be recognized so that clinically important treatment threats and benefits can be detected. Conflict exists regarding what may be viewed as credible evidence for a meta-analysis. The National Health Service Centre for Reviews and Dissemination (2001) argue that randomized control trials contain the best available evidence and therefore should always be used where possible. However, there is strong evidence that this form of thinking is fading and additional 'softer' types of evidence are gaining approval, although some authors (Jenson and Allen 1994; Sandelowski et al. 1997) argue that where softer research is used the title 'meta-synthesis' should be used. Manzoni et al. (2008) used a meta-analysis to investigate the efficacy of relaxation in the treatment of anxiety and used only randomized control trials which resulted in a small number of studies, only 27 in total, meeting the inclusion and exclusion criteria.

The strengths of the systematic review and meta-analysis are rooted in their ability to reduce bias and error, however their credibility can be impacted by the quality of the underlying studies; some authors refer to this as the GIGO principle (garbage in, garbage out). Healthcare practitioners are at the mercy of these reviewers and researchers, hence, even seemingly dependable sources of evidence must be viewed with caution and an open mind. Meta-analysis is not suitable for novice researchers as a comprehensive knowledge of statistics and the ability to critique are required.

Audit

Audit is part of the clinical governance framework through which organizations are accountable for the quality of their provision. It is a cycle of continuous improvement that has equity, accessibility and acceptability as important considerations. Audit is concerned with improving quality in health care through improved working practices, improved health outcomes or the improved use of resources. It is evaluative and reflective and often involves change. Although both audit and research can be concerned with reviewing practice, planning change and implementing improvements, Bowling (2009) refers to research as distinct from audit as they differ in their aims and outcomes. Audit is described as a management function and tends to be rooted in a specific strategic direction. It is concerned with analysing existing data, monitoring standards and evaluating service delivery whereas research is described as deriving generalizable new data. Bowling (2009) argues that, unlike research, audit does not contribute to a scientific body of knowledge in that its aim is to maintain quality rather than the creation of new worlds or patterns of thinking. In other words, research is finding out what you should be doing, audit is finding out if you are doing it and whether it is working. The process of audit can be summarized in the audit cycle in Figure 2.3. Audit

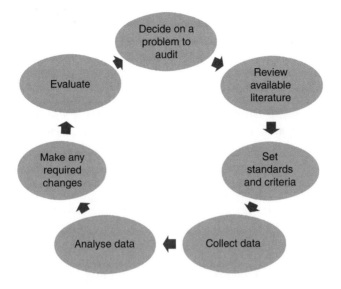

Figure 2.3   The audit process.

is depicted as a continual process unlike research, which is often carried out to its conclusion.

There are similarities between research and audit; for example, audit utilizes some research methods such as focus groups, surveys, literature reviewing, statistical analysis and clinical case reviews. In this way, it could be acknowledged as a scientific endeavour, in that it employs a systematic process, has measurable outcomes, has predictive end points, is transparent and non-judgemental, and has ethical considerations in reducing harm. However, unlike research audit does not usually need approval by local or central ethics committees and is therefore an attractive alternative to research.

Types of research: the quantitative/qualitative debate

This chapter has so far defined the nature of research and differentiated between research and non-research. Research has been defined as planned action that systematically investigates a question or topic by sampling a population and reporting the results. Some research requires ethical approval and all research should comply with ethical principles. In contrast non-research does not usually require ethical approval, does not sample populations and may involve analysing literature rather than interacting with people. Just when we think that we have clarified what research is and are able to define the characteristics of research another dilemma presents itself as there are opposing schools of thought about what constitutes legitimate research knowledge. The next section will discuss the types of research that exist and the steps involved in the research process.

Paradigms

The research world comprises of multiple belief systems, much like the rest of the outside world. These belief systems have influenced the development of research styles and practices referred to as 'paradigms'. Denzin and Lincoln (1994) refer to a paradigm as a set of beliefs that guide action by providing a particular view of the world which, then, shapes the way that we interpret and understand our environment. Two particular paradigms dominate the research arena: the positivist or quantitative paradigm which adopts a hard science approach and the naturalist or qualitative paradigm that is considered softer and less scientific. Each of these paradigms will be explored in more depth in Chapters 3, 4, 5 and 6; in this section they are merely introduced.

Each research paradigm is rooted in a set of theoretical assumptions about how health care should be investigated and what may be perceived as 'true'. Researchers often take these paradigms to the extreme, adopting fixed and inflexible positions The very fact that these polarized positions exist should raise the question 'is there actually any truth?' as if any one of these positions were true there would not be the opportunity for debate. Cormack (2000) claims that the human dilemma is to be forever held captive by myths as reality can never be mastered. The battle for dominance is futile as each paradigm has its purpose and place according to the research question. Furthermore, having these opportunities for debate makes research more vibrant and interesting. Healthcare issues often have quantitative and qualitative dimensions, for example, obtaining a blood pressure could be perceived as quantitative as it involves numbers and is an objective form of measurement; however, to take a blood pressure in a caring way that considers the patient's feelings and meaning is a qualitative skill. Another example where quantitative and qualitative elements are mixed could be to consider the case of Betty in the example below:

Example

Thirty experiments were carried out to test the efficacy of dressing X. The results showed that, when compared with other dressings, healing rates were increased when it is used on the lower leg. Betty has a wound on her lower leg and her nurse advises Betty that this will be a good dressing to use. The nurse explains the results of the experiments to Betty in the hope that she will also believe in the evidence. However, the dressing is large and very visible. Betty states that she likes to have her legs exposed in the summer and needs to feel pretty. She chooses an alternative dressing that is transparent but is limited in its effectiveness.

When discussing the merits of the narrative approach to research, Carson and Fairbairn (2002) stated:

'While research in wound healing might provide evidence for the efficacy of a particular dressing over others, awareness of the lifestyle of a patient, gained by listening to their stories, might suggest that the optimum treatment would be another dressing that they are more likely to tolerate.'

This statement demonstrates that while quantitative research based evidence such as that from experiments can be useful in guiding clinical decision making sometimes the qualitative perceptions of the patient are more important to the reality of healthcare.

Consider the above statements about wound care; can you see both sides of the argument? Should Betty use dressing X as it the most effective treatment option? Your decision will depend upon what you believe to be most important, scientific evidence or personal preference.

The debate as to the most appropriate approach for researchers is meaningless as each methodology has its merits and detriments. Research is more than the technical use of processes, it is about applying the most appropriate methods to understand a situation or solve a problem. Carson and Fairbairn (2002) add that quantitative and qualitative paradigms need to be evaluated against the standard of their ability to help people while Bowling (2009) suggests that the choice of research approach should depend upon the type of question to be answered. In order to decide which paradigm is most preferable to you, the paradigms should be explored in more depth. The key elements of each paradigm will be discussed in the next section.

Quantitative research

Quantitative research is often referred to as the scientific paradigm as it is systematic in its approach and uses statistics to analyse the data. A key feature of quantitative research is the attempt to eliminate bias through the process of objectivity. This involves strategies to limit the extent to which the researcher is able to manipulate the findings through their role as researcher. The characteristics of quantitative research are summarized below and are discussed in depth in Chapters 3 and 4:

- Quantitative reality is derived deductively from existing knowledge, based upon the assumption that for every effect there is a cause and that this cause will hold true if the situation were to be repeated under the same conditions.
- Quantitative research relies heavily on quantification and assigns a numerical value to any matter worthy of study.

- Quantitative research only accepts that which is observable and measureable as legitimate; for example, feelings cannot be measured and therefore are not accepted as real.
- Quantitative research seeks to measure phenomena in a numerical, objective fashion in order that propositions can be empirically verified or denied.
- The goal is to establish universal laws common to phenomena regardless of their setting.

In contrast, the qualitative paradigm:

- adopts an inductive approach to generate theory after the collection of data;
- believes that the social world is not fixed so cannot be predicted as people are free agents within it, hence, universal laws cannot be legitimate as people cannot be controlled;
- believes that it is impossible to be objective as people interpret their world in a subjective way, therefore, descriptions of experience rather than numbers are more valid forms of knowledge;
- believes that people should be studied in their natural environments where possible as the context has relevance to the experience being described;
- uses small numbers of participants in the study in order to collect in-depth, detailed experiences;
- analyses the material gathered in terms of words and phrases.

The research process

As already stated, in order to be perceived as scientific, both quantitative and qualitative research paradigms need to follow a systematic process. The research process refers to an orderly series of steps or phases which act as a framework to legitimize the study. The steps appear to occur in an ordered linear manner; however, many researchers acknowledge that far from being organized the process can sometimes be messy and unpredictable. For example, stages often overlap and the researcher may have to shift back and forth between phases especially if problems arise with issues concerning reliability and validity. There are some commonsense tasks that must be carried out sequentially; for example, one cannot analyse data until it has been collected. Several models exist to guide novice researchers through the research process. Each of these has a different number of stages and uses different terminology; however, providing that the central tasks are carried out, the variance is

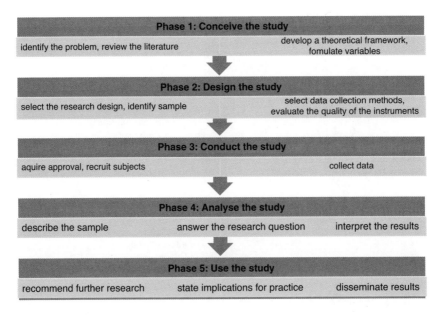

Phase 1: Conceive the study

identify the problem, review the literature   develop a theoretical framework,
                                                           fomulate variables

Phase 2: Design the study

select the research design, identify sample   select data collection methods,
                                                          evaluate the quality of the instruments

Phase 3: Conduct the study

aquire approval, recruit subjects   collect data

Phase 4: Analyse the study

describe the sample   answer the research question   interpret the results

Phase 5: Use the study

recommend further research   state implications for practice   disseminate results

Figure 2.4   Stages in the quantitative research process.

irrelevant. Borbasi et al. (2004) identified five stages to the quantitative re-search process (see Figure 2.4).

From Figure 2.4 we can see that stages one and two are the thinking and reading segments of the research process; these stages focus the research by reviewing what is already known, formulating a framework and devising the hypothesis that is to be tested. In these phases, decisions are made about how to conduct the study and the methods that will be employed; this is known as the 'research design'.

Phase three is the active part of the process where the research design is implemented and the data is collected. It is often the most problematic and least predictive element of a study as it involves real people in real contexts.

The fourth phase is considered the most meaningful part of the process as results are analysed and interpreted. The researcher makes sense of the findings and puts them into context in order to answer the research question or accept or reject the hypothesis. Relationships are verified and explanations are proposed.

Phase five is perhaps the most crucial part of the research process as the results are shared with the research consumers and the implications for practice are realized. Sometimes studies can be small scale and require fur-ther studies or may reveal further problems that require investigation, hence recommendations are made. This implies a circular nature to the research process. The same researcher may not be involved but this notion complies

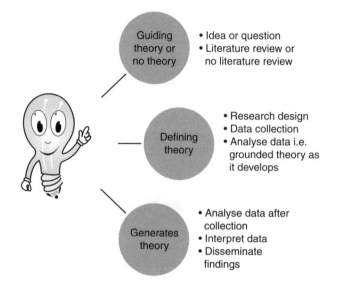

Figure 2.5 The qualitative research process.

with Cormack's statement that the world can never be mastered as there are always opportunities for further research to support or refute previous work.

The qualitative research process

The qualitative research process is often more flexible and less sequential than the quantitative process in that phases often occur simultaneously or have to be revisited; for example in the grounded theory approach, data is analysed as it is gathered and is compared with previous data using the 'constant comparative method'. This often involves the researcher having to revisit participants to qualify or validate their discussions. The stages of the research process may differ from one study to another and a variety of approaches and techniques may be used. The research may or may not have a theory guiding the study; a literature review may be conducted at the start of the study, at the end of the study or not at all if there is no existing data. An example of the qualitative research process could be as shown in Figure 2.5.

Although the qualitative research process appears to be more relaxed and flexible compared to the quantitative research process, this is not actually the case. Both research approaches must be systematic in order to be considered scientific. Qualitative research must meet strict standards of rigour if it is to be accepted as robust evidence; for example the theory underpinning the research must be explicit, sampling procedures must be clearly rationalized and the analysis must adhere to recognized procedures.

Summary

The purpose of this chapter is to clarify the nature of research for the reader in order to establish a foundation for further understanding of research culture. Research has been defined as a process of enquiry that is systematic, critical and practical. Some researchers have argued that research should be purposeful and directly applied to healthcare outcomes in order to develop theory and create innovation. Alternatively, some researchers have argued that research can be used to satisfy curiosity about the nature of the world around us and need not have any directly observable health benefits. These diverse views show that the purpose of research has not been clearly defined and remains an issue for debate.

Two distinct ways of thinking have been identified and have been linked to the two dominant research paradigms. Quantitative research has been linked to deductive reasoning and has been described as a hard science approach to investigation. This approach assumes that all reality is measurable and predictable in order to establish laws and patterns. Alternatively qualitative research adopts an inductive approach and uses descriptions of experiences to understand the world. This type of research assumes that people are free agents and cannot be predicted but can be understood. Each paradigm has been described as useful and the debate as to which one should predominate is meaningless as each one needs to be evaluated according to the nature of the research question and the ability to enhance understanding.

Reflective activity

- Identify a problem from practice that you feel could be either understood better or managed more effectively through the use of a research study.
- Which research paradigm would you use to investigate the problem?
- Consider what factors made you arrive at that decision.
- What are the advantages of your chosen approach and what stages would you use to guide you through the research process?
- Do you see any potential barriers or problems in your approach?

Jargon busting

Make a list of any words in this chapter that you do not understand. Look up their meaning and consider their use in the world of research. You may identify some of the following words and terms.

Analysis: Data is scrutinized to determine its meaning.

Demographics: Statistics used to define a population.

Hypothesis: A testable statement that makes a prediction about two or more factors.

Paradigm: A set of philosophical assumptions that underpin a process of enquiry.

Qualitative research: A soft science approach to research that uses induction, interpretation and experience to formulate theory.

Quantitative research: A hard science approach to research that uses numerical data to measure information about the world in order to predict and explain causal events.

Research: A systematic process of enquiry that uses induction and deduction to confirm existing knowledge and generate new knowledge. It can be applied or pure.

Systematic: A methodical process that uses various sequential stages.

Theoretical framework: The theoretical foundation that guides the research study.

References

Benner, P. and Wrubel, J. (1989) *The Primacy of Caring: Stress and Coping in Health and Illness*. Menlo Park, CA: Addison-Wesley.

Bernstein, R.J. (1983) *Beyond Objectivism and Relativism*. Philadelphia: University of Pennsylvania Press.

Borbasi, S., Jackson, D., Langford, R.W. (2004) *Navigating the Maze of Nursing Research: An Interactive Adventure*. London: Mosby.

Bowling, A. (2009) *Research Methods in Health: Investigating Health and Health Services*. Maidenhead: Open University Press.

Burns, N. and Grove, S.K. (2005) *The Practice of Nursing Research: Conduct, Critique and Utilization*, 5th edn. St Louis, MI: Elsevier Saunders.

Carson, A.M. and Fairbairn, G.J. (2002) The whole story: towards an ethical research methodology, *Nurse Researcher*, 10(1): 15–29.

Cormack, D.F. (2000) *The Research Process in Nursing*. London: Blackwell Science Ltd.

Denzin, N.K. and Lincoln, Y.S. (1994) *The Handbook of Qualitative Research*. CA: Sage.

Frascati Manual (1993) *Proposed Standard Practice for Surveys on Research and Experimental Development*. Paris: OECD.

Jenson, L.A. and Allen, M.N. (1994) A synthesis of qualitative research on wellness-illness, *Qualitative Health Research*, 4(4): 349–69.

Lacey, A. (1999) Perceptions of research. Cited In: Mulhall, A. Le May, A. (1999) *Nursing research. Dissemination and implementation.* London: Churchill Livingstone.

Lewis, R.A., Russell, D., Hughes, D.A. et al. (2009) Patients' and healthcare professionals' views of cancer follow up: a systematic review, *British Journal of General Practice*, 59: 248–59.

Manzoni, G.M., Pagini, F., Castelnuovo, G. and Molinari, E. (2008) Meta-analysis into the effectiveness of relaxation as a treatment for anxiety, *BMC Psychiatry*, 8(14): 14.

Macleod Clark, J. and Hockey, L. (1989) *Further Research for Nursing*. London: Soutari Press.

McVicar, A. (2003) Workplace stress in nursing: a literature review, *Journal of Advanced Nursing*, 44(6): 633–42.

Morrison, P. and Burnard, P. (1997) *Caring and Communication: The Interpersonal Relationship in Nursing*. London: MacMillan Press.

Mulhall, A., and Le May, A. (1999) *Nursing Research: Dissemination and Implementation*. London: Churchill Livingstone.

Mulrow, C.D., Cook, D.J. and Davidoff, F. (1997) Systematic review: critical links in the chain of evidence, *Annals of internal medicine*, 126(5): 389–91.

National Health Service Centre for Reviews and Dissemination (2001) York: York University.

Orpen, N. and Harris, J. (2010) Perceptions of preoperative home-based occupational therapy and/or physiotherapy interventions prior to total hip replacement, *British Journal of Occupational Therapy*, 73(10): 461–8.

Parahoo, K. (2006) *Nursing Research: Principles, Process and Issues*. Basingstoke Hampshire: Palgrave Macmillan.

Robson, C. (2002) *Real World Research: A Resource for Social Scientists and Practitioner-researchers*. London: Blackwell.

Ross, T. (2000) A phenomenological study into the meaning of caring. Unpublished thesis, Glyndwr University, Wrexham, Wales.

Sandelowski, M., Docherty, S. and Emden, C. (1997) Qualitative meta-synthesis: issues and techniques, *Research in Nursing and Health*, 20: 365–71.

Sridhar, M.S. (2010) *Introduction to Research Methodology*. http://www.slideshare. net/mssidhar/introduction-to-research-methodology (accessed 13 July 2010).

Tatum, M. (2003) *What is applied research?* http: //www.wisegeek.com/what-is-applied-research.htm (accessed 6 August 2010).

Victor, E. (2009) *A Systematic Review of Interventions for Carers in the United Kingdom: Outcomes and Exploratory Evidence*. Essex: Princess Royal Trust for Carers.

Waters, C. (2009) *The romance of pure research*. http://www.povatdhi.wordpress. com/2009/10/06.the-romance-of-pure-research/ (accessed 13 July 2010).

Watson, J. (1979) *Nursing: The Philosophy and Science of Caring*. Boston, MA: Little, Brown.

3 Quantitative research

Introduction

In the previous chapter you were introduced to the notion of research paradigms which were described as ways of thinking about how knowledge can be obtained. This chapter builds on material covered in Chapter 2 and explores the quantitative paradigm in more depth. From personal experience many students express confusion between the terms quantitative and qualitative research; my response has been to advise students to think about quantitative research in terms of 'quantity' which infers numbers and measurement, the other type then must be qualitative.

As mentioned in the previous chapter, both quantitative and qualitative paradigms aim to determine the truth about the world that we live in and, as stated, what exists as truth is debatable. However, the researcher's philosophical standpoint is crucial as it impinges upon the selection of research methods and the types of topics that will be investigated. Developing an understanding of the philosophical basis of quantitative research will help you to comprehend the structures that direct the quantitative research process and appreciate the appropriateness of different data gathering methods that exist. The knowledge that you gain from this chapter will help you to differentiate between quantitative and qualitative styles of research and critically appreciate their similarities and differences. It will also enable you to consider how and when you would use each style to solve healthcare problems and enhance understanding of health and illness.

Learning outcomes

At the end of this chapter you will be able to:

- discuss the historical context of quantitative research;
- identify the key features of quantitative research;

- define the term post-positivism;
- differentiate between the different types of hypotheses and variables;
- demonstrate an awareness of sampling techniques used in quantitative research;
- describe the methods of data collection used in quantitative research;
- evaluate the strengths and weaknesses of quantitative research.

Historical context and key features of quantitative research

Philosophy has a relevance to research as it makes explicit the principles and beliefs that underpin particular modes of investigation. Each research paradigm has a philosophical base that guides the direction of the research. Quantitative research emerged from a branch of philosophy called positivism. Positivism has been the dominant mode of thinking from the ancient Greeks to modern day. The most prominent positivists appear to be Auguste Comte (1798–1857) who is regarded as the first philosopher of science and Emile Durkheim (1858–1917) who is famous for comparing the suicide rates between Catholics and Protestants. It is believed that quantitative psychology was first introduced by Gustav Fechner (1801–1887), a German psychologist who examined the relationship between psychological sensation and the intensity of a stimulus. In the UK, John Snow was accredited with undertaking the first epidemiological study when in 1854 he established that an outbreak of cholera was linked to a water pump.

The principles of positivism remain prevalent in modern healthcare research, for example the randomized control trial is still regarded by the Centre for Research and Dissemination as the gold standard. Within health care, quantitative research appears to have gained more prestige than qualitative research as it is considered more scientific and trustworthy and therefore has tended to make a greater impact upon healthcare policy and interventions. Research carried out by Hunter and Leahey (2008) found that between 1935 and 2005 at least two thirds of all sociological research carried out adopted a positivist stance.

What is positivism?

Positivism has four key features:

- objectivity;
- only measurable phenomena exist;
- all people are similar and react in the same ways to stimuli;
- there is an absolute reality that can be measured.

Each of these four features will be discussed.

Objectivity

Positivism is based upon the tenet that only that which is directly observable and testable can be accepted as valid knowledge. Any data that can be objectively measured is acknowledged as real; for example, the recording of blood pressures, the number of times that a particular disease presents itself within a community or that if a person sits in the same position for a prolonged period of time their skin will break down. This implies that subjective phenomena such as feelings and experiences are not considered valid as they are not amenable to measurement, they may be observable but need to be interpreted to be meaningful. It is difficult to apply numerical levels to feelings hence they cannot be reliably analysed through the use of statistics.

The quantitative research paradigm has traditionally been perceived as the scientific method of research as knowledge is generated through the application of logical principles and reasoning. A strict systematic process is followed and the researcher adopts a distant and non-interactive stance to the data in order to reduce any element of bias that could impact the potential truth of the findings. In this way, it is perceived as objective as the researcher is not seen. Quantitative researchers believe that truth can be distorted and measurement can be contaminated through the influence of feelings, perceptions and values.

In quantitative research the researcher uses control to limit the influence of any external factors that could impact the results of the study; in this way the world can be 'reduced' into parts that can be manipulated or held constant in order to view their impact. This explains why many critics refer to quantitative research as 'reductionist'. However, Gouldner (1991) refers to the mythical minotaur, half man and half bull, to argue that man and bull cannot be separated. By this, he implies that the researcher cannot be separated from their values and personal biography as these values have directed the researcher in the choice of topic, the type of research style and what is perceived as valuable. Bowling (2009) agrees and adds that scientists cannot divorce themselves from their cultural, social and political contexts and should instead make their assumptions explicit so that their values can be evaluated as part of the research process. Mitroff (1974) claimed that scientists themselves agree that the notion of pure objectivity is ingenuous and states that: 'In order to be a good scientist, one has to have biases. The best scientist, not only has a point of view but defends it with gusto. The scientist does not cheat by falsifying data but does everything in his power to defend his hypothesis against the introduction of fluke data.' (p. 1)

Coolican (2004) argued that it is naive to assume that one could ever gather data without some background theory in our heads and adds that when we perceive the world we inevitably go beyond the information given. This implies that even when one tries to be objective, as data is obtained, some unconscious analysis is taking place; we subconsciously try to ascertain how the information fits with the world as we know it in order to make it meaningful. Mulhall and Le May (1999) support this line of thinking by adding that all knowledge is socially constructed and cannot be disentangled from the world in which it is created.

Exercise 3.1

Consider the above paragraph for a moment. Do you think that it is possible for a researcher to be objective in the research process? Is it important to be objective? Why? Why not? How do you think that a researcher can promote objectivity in a research project? How can objectivity be compromised? This is a lot to consider but may help you adopt a critical stance when evaluating the different research paradigms.

Only measurable phenomena exist

Positivism measures data statistically through the use of numbers. If it can't be measured, it does not exist. Mathematics has proved its place in the world of health care and many problems have been solved using the principles of science; for example, disease rates have been established through the use of statistics, mathematical formulary have been applied to develop drugs and therapies and healthcare policy is dominated by the numerical voting process. An easy way to remember this is to think 'that which is countable, counts!'

All people are similar and react in the same way to stimuli

Positivism assumes that all human behaviour is reactional, in response to external stimuli. This view perceives humans as identical closed systems which enables them to be predicted and explained using the principles of science in order to create universal laws. Such a view assumes first that the world is static and second that all humans will react in the same way in similar situations. Humans are seen as simplistic and mechanistic. This view fails to consider cultural interpretations, technological disturbances and human anarchy that may exist in normal societies.

There is an absolute reality that can be measured

Positivism holds the belief that absolute truth exists and that this truth is discoverable and measurable. It is derived deductively from existing knowledge, based upon the assumption that for every effect there exists a cause and that the cause is amenable to objective evaluation. However, this theory assumes that truly objective tools of measurement exist, for example a watch will only tell the correct time if it has a working battery and is set at the correct time when it is purchased; additionally, a sphygmomanometer that is used to measure blood pressure needs constant calibration and may run out of battery life.

Exercise 3.2

Consider the following tools. How objective and potentially accurate do you believe them to be? What factors could impact their reliability?

- a set of weighing scales
- the Edinburgh Depression rating scale
- a tympanic thermometer
- a digital blood pressure monitor
- a speedometer in a car

Post-positivism

Modern positivists acknowledge that some of the traditional positivist notions are too naive and idealistic to solve modern healthcare problems and this has led to the creation of a new post-positive movement sometimes referred to as critical realism. The most famous post-positivist is Karl Popper whose theories became popular in the 1960s. The term 'post' indicates a further development of the original theory. Post-positivism has retained many of the original positivist ideals such as the belief in deduction and quantification but has some quite significant changes in its suppositions and may be considered positivism in a moderated form.

While qualitative research tends to be inductive and quantitative research tends to be deductive, post-positivism refers to itself as 'retroductive' which focuses on why events occur in the way that they do. Post-positivists accept that establishing absolute reality may be too unrealistic and instead accept that the aim of quantitative research is really to discover what is probable given the knowledge that currently exists. They have moved away from trying to create universal laws to explain behaviour and instead highlight what is most plausible. Therefore, they aim to get as close as possible to the truth. Instead of establishing cause and effect they seek to examine correlations or relationships between phenomena. They believe that healthcare outcomes have causative factors that interact with each other. The notion that the world can be observed in a detached manner is also questioned by post-positivists and instead the focus is centred on creating tools that enhance objectivity and reduce as much bias as possible.

Quantitative research methodology

Research methodology is concerned with the planning, design and implementation of strategies to gather and analyse data (Sheehan 1986). Four centuries ago Descartes (1637) is quoted as stating: 'In the search for truth of things method is indispensable.' Descartes implies that how the results are achieved is sometimes far more important that the findings themselves as this is a journey of discovery. The hallmark of a good piece of quantitative research lies in the attention given to the research methodology and the reliability of the tools that are used to acquire data. This next section will discuss the components of quantitative research and the methods used to acquire data.

There are generally two forms of quantitative research design: experimental and non-experimental (commonly referred to as ex-post-facto).

- In non-experimental research the work tends to be exploratory where the researcher studies existing situations and reports the findings. Examples would be the use of a survey to investigate patient satisfaction levels. Non-experimental research tends to provide descriptive data that can be used for predictive purposes.
- Experimental research is used to establish cause and effect to deduce higher levels of prediction. For example, if a researcher wants to investigate whether a particular drug will reduce pain, they may construct an experiment that tests several different drugs against each other or use the same drug on several different patients.

Most quantitative studies start with either a research question that has to be answered by the data or with a hypothesis that is accepted or rejected.

The research question

Research questions are the specific queries that researchers want to answer in order to address a problem (Polit and Beck 2010). The research question is the fundamental driving force for any research as it justifies the activity, focuses the topic and determines the methods of data collection. The question needs to be specific and should establish a clear purpose for the study such as filling a gap in knowledge or solving a healthcare problem. It should be currently relevant as it provides a framework for the rest of the study. Fads will not stand the test of time and become dated very quickly.

The question is often formulated as a result of a literature review and is problem specific. Burns and Grove (2006) state that a well-formulated research question can generate numerous research problems and direct a lifetime of research activities. Research questions should be interesting and motivational if they are to stimulate further research studies. For example, there is no point choosing a question that has already been answered by many other researchers such as 'What causes pressure ulcers?' or 'Does chocolate eaten in large proportions influence weight gain?'. The questions should also be feasible and achievable. For example, the question 'Can we save the world?' is not achievable as the world is too large to consider saving and the question is not focused enough. However, if we were to pose the question 'Can physiotherapists in Wales reduce the number of falls at home through the use of correctly measured Zimmer frames?' this is far more focused and achievable.

Exercise 3.3

From the following list of research questions identify which questions are broad, narrow or reasonable questions to research. The answers are provided in the Appendix:

1   How important is exercise?
2   What are the stages of the audit cycle?
3   What types of attitudes do healthcare professionals have towards mental health patients?
4   What infection control procedures did nurses use in the past?
5   Do boys or girls have the largest vocabularies?
6   Can the introduction of classical music reduce anxiety levels in preoperative patients?
7   What do health providers think are important?

Creating a hypothesis

A hypothesis is used to test the soundness of a theory and encourages the process of logical thought as researchers critically consider why particular events occur. Second, the hypothesis gives focus to the study; for example, imagine if a study just tried to answer the following question: what causes stress in patients? There are many options that the researcher could choose to explore and the research could potentially have no end point. Alternatively, if the researcher decided to choose one or more aspects to explore and then tested each of these, the research would be more achievable and have more direction. For example: placing patients in mixed bay wards causes stress in patients. A hypothesis basically makes a prediction about the expected outcome and is written in the form of a testable statement. A hypothesis is always written in the future tense as it occurs prior to the study. One could say that the hypothesis is about making educated guesses or inferences about causal connections. It does not try to explain why or offer solutions, it merely predicts the outcome.

An example of a hypothesis:

You notice that you have developed a rash on your abdomen; you have recently changed washing powder so you make an educated guess that there is a causal connection between the soap powder and the rash. If this were written as a hypothesis it would state:

When used to wash clothes soap powder XX will cause a local rash on the human abdomen.

A hypothesis is concerned with establishing plausible relationships between factors. The hypothesis is derived from existing theory, for example it may be arrived at after a literature review, as the result of experience or from an untested idea. The hypothesis is tested and then accepted or rejected. A good hypothesis is testable not necessarily provable. So if we return to the washing powder, you could now try washing with several different powders and review the results. If the rash is only present when powder XX is used we may accept the hypothesis. If the rash is present with all of the powders we may reject the hypothesis and consider additional potential causes, i.e. viral illness, allergy to clothing, materials, etc.

Knowledge is accumulated through the process of either verification or falsification as the surviving theory occupies a position of primacy until a stronger theory is generated. The survival of a hypothesis relies upon consensus from additional studies. This is known as the hypothetico-deductive method. Some may argue that rather than being scientific, this method relies very much upon trial and error knowledge which is high risk and difficult to audit trail. Furthermore, Coolican (2004) argues that for every single supportive piece of evidence there is very often an alternative explanation and Popper (1959) stated that for any theory to count as theory we must be able to perceive how it could possibly be falsified. Several types of hypothesis are used in quantitative research; each of these will be discussed.

A loose hypothesis

A loose hypothesis is defined as a very unspecific and weak hypothesis that is too vague for testing by research. An example could be: boys are better readers than girls. This type of hypothesis fails to state the ages of the groups, no tools are used to test the assumption and no details about the groups under study are offered.

A research hypothesis

This is the most typical hypothesis used in research studies as it is specific enough to be testable. For example:

When presented with the level three book, *Janet meet Jane,* a cohort of 10-year-old boys will be able to verbalize more written words than a cohort of 10-year-old girls.

We can see that, compared with the loose hypothesis, there are details about the groups and the tools for measurement are specified, which make the comparison more accurate.

Directional hypothesis

A directional hypothesis or one-tailed hypothesis is used when the direction of the effect is stated so the effect will be in the direction of a high result or a low result. For example: students who receive two or more tutorials for an assignment will achieve higher grades than those students who only attend for one tutorial. This type of hypothesis is used when the researcher has substantive knowledge about the topic area and is easily able to make a prediction about the result.

Non-directional hypothesis

A non-directional hypothesis is often referred to as a two-tailed hypothesis and is used when the direction of the effect is not stated. For example: there is a relationship between the number of tutorials received by students and the results that they achieve. This type of hypothesis is used when the researcher has no clear idea of the nature of the relationship but assumes that one exists. Some researchers argue that a non-directional hypothesis should be used where possible as they suggest impartiality whereas a directional hypothesis commits the researcher towards an outcome and may lead to bias. Others argue that a directional hypothesis demonstrates that the researcher has critically explored the relevant theory that exists in order to make a more accurate prediction.

Null hypothesis

A null hypothesis or statistical hypothesis predicts the absence of a relationship between the factors under investigation. It states that any observed changes are due to chance and not the variables under investigation. An example of a null hypothesis would be: there is no relationship between the number of tutorials undertaken by students and the results that they achieve, or: oxygen inhalation via nasal cannula of up to 6 litres per minute does not affect oral temperature when measured with an electronic thermometer. If the null hypothesis is rejected, it does not follow that the research hypothesis is automatically accepted, it merely demonstrates that there is insufficient support for the null hypothesis. Researchers have different beliefs about when to use a research hypothesis and when to use a null hypothesis. The null hypothesis is often preferred when there is insufficient theory upon which to predict a positive relationship; others claim that it is easier to interpret the statistical results and some researchers state both, for example Cheng et al. (2002) stated both when they investigated the consistency of self-reported blood pressures.

Complex hypothesis

A complex hypothesis predicts the relationship between three or more factors. An example of a complex hypothesis would be Rawl et al.'s (2002) study into the effects of a computer based nursing intervention upon psychological functioning, depression rating scores and anxiety levels. The hypothesis was written as 'patients with cancer who received a computer based nursing intervention will have higher psychological functioning scores and lower depression scores and anxiety rating scores'. In this study the psychological functioning scores did not support the hypothesis but the anxiety level ratings and the depression ratings did support the hypothesis. Another example could be: eating large proportions of high calorie foods will result in obesity, Type 2 diabetes and exogenous depression. The advantage of using a complex hypothesis reduces the need for several separate studies saving time and resources.

Identifying hypotheses

In a quantitative research study the hypothesis may not be explicitly stated; it may be embedded in the literature for you to discover. If the hypothesis is not explicitly stated, you should consider why this is the case and whether its absence is justified. Sometimes there is no theory available and the researchers are not able to predict an outcome; occasionally the hypothesis may have no logical connection to current knowledge and sometimes they are written so poorly that they bear little resemblance to the nature of enquiry. Good research students should have some knowledge about what constitutes a high-quality hypothesis in order to evaluate the credibility of quantitative research studies. LoBiondo-Wood and Haber (2010) state that a high-quality hypothesis is explicit, has clear relationship statements, is testable, identifies the population and the variables are clearly defined.

Exercise 3.4

Identify which of following hypotheses are: loose, research, directional, non-directional and complex. Note that they may have more than one characteristic, i.e. be loose and non-directional. The answers are provided in the Appendix.

1   Chocolate causes spots.
2   People will make more errors on a flight simulator in noisy conditions than in quiet conditions.
3   There will be a difference in the frequency of memory lapses among people aged 29–39 than in people aged 50–59 years of age.
4   Temperature affects mood.
5   Absence makes the heart grow fonder.
6   There will be a difference in the time a person takes to respond to an emergency depending upon whether they are alone or not.
7   When using the Ross stress testing instrument, there will be a positive correlation between the self-reported stress levels of healthcare professionals and the implementation of the Type 3 Vant Swedish massage programme.
8   There will be no relationship between the mortality rates of patients receiving care in ITU and patients receiving care in CCU.
9   Drinking three cups of coffee over a period of three hours will reduce self-reported fatigue levels, reduce the number of self-reported headaches and increase self-reported concentration levels.

Sampling for quantitative research

The most reliable and valid study would probably be one in which every person in the world is able to participate but of course this is unreasonable as resources would soon be depleted and not every member of society may be suitable for the particular study. Furthermore, analysing the data would result in superficial explanations and exceed the lifespan of most researchers. In response, researchers have to resort to strategies that permit them to obtain data from smaller groups that can be generalized back to the larger population. This process is called sampling.

Sampling is the process of selecting suitable subjects for participation into a study. A *sample* is a subset of a population that is selected for inclusion into a study and is expressed as: n = number. A *population* may be defined as the total number of individuals or units from which data can potentially be drawn.

The *target population* or the *sampling frame* is the group that the researcher aims to select the sample from. These are the people of interest to the researcher. Sometimes all the members of the target population are included in the study; this is termed *total population sampling* and is often used where potential subjects are limited. An example could be where a small number of people have experienced a particular phenomenon or a number of people exhibit particular disease symptoms.

There are two key considerations when sampling is used in quantitative studies; these are to ensure that samples are:

- **representative:** this refers to the extent to which the sample reflect the characteristics of the normal population; for example, the sample should contain proportionate numbers of males and females, represent people from across the life span, contain people from multiple ethnic groups, etc. It is important that the sample selected is representative of the general population so that generalizations can be made. For example, if the researcher seeks to study people's perceptions of violence on TV the sample should not just comprise of people with violent backgrounds or the results will be skewed;
- **homogeneous:** this refers to the extent to which the sample are similar in their characteristics. For example, if a researcher claims to be sampling occupational therapists they should possess the qualities that one would expect from occupational therapists and not be uniquely different.

Two types of sampling are used in quantitative research: probability and non-probability. Probability sampling enables the researcher to make inferences about populations and enables the results of the study to be calculated statistically but it is reliant upon accessing a large number of participants. In contrast, non-probability sampling tends to use samples that fit the purpose of the study or are selected for the sake of convenience.

Probability sampling or random sampling

This is the most common form of sampling in a quantitative study and is highly regarded for its potential rigour. This method involves numbering all of the potential subjects in a study. The subjects are then selected through the use of a lottery or a random number table. Often computer assisted tables are used as this reduces the potential for researcher bias. For example, *systematic random sampling* can be used to select every tenth member of a group. Systematic sampling ensures that every member of the target population has the potential to be selected; however, this has the potential to result in a very unrepresentative sample. For example, it may be that every tenth member happens to be female or under the age of 25 or unmarried. Although people with these characteristics are present in normal society they do not represent a normal society and, therefore, would not be representative. This has serious consequences for the study as the researcher cannot be confident that the results can be applied to larger populations and it cannot be used to reliably establish laws and truths. A representative sample is one whose key characteristics closely approximate those of the general population.

The researcher also has to be sure that every member in the sample group has the characteristics that are being studied. For example, if you wanted to know whether cornflakes cause hyperactivity in children, every participant in the study needs to have eaten cornflakes or the study would be considered unreliable and have limited validity.

The second problem for random sampling concerns the size of the required sample. As a general rule of thumb, the larger the population, the greater the chance of representation. Most researchers advise that any study with a sample of less than 30 should be viewed with caution (Borbasi et al. 2004). It is important to consider that limited exposure to people = limited exposure to data. A statistical test called a power analysis is used to determine if the sample size is adequate and in a good study this figure should be evident and the sample size should be justified (power analysis will be discussed in more detail in Chapter 4).

As healthcare research impacts those who are the most vulnerable in society it is important that the results are as reliable as possible. Selecting subjects randomly has ethical implications; for example, should vulnerable people be included? Is there any potential for harm? If they are excluded, would the result be an unrepresentative sample? However, as the numbers used are large, the reliability of the study is impacted less if subjects are withdrawn. The major disadvantage of random sampling is that it is time-consuming and expensive and therefore other less expensive methods may be used such as stratified sampling or quota sampling.

Stratified random sampling is used when the researcher wants to ensure that each group in a society is represented. Specific numbers of subjects who possess the same characteristics are selected and the sample is then divided into subgroups. The groups are subdivided according to the characteristics required. For example, the researcher decides upon several types of strict eligibility criteria and recruits until the required quota has been met. For example, the researcher may decide that they want to sample 25 males aged between 20 and 39 years, 25 males aged between 40 and 50 years and 10 males aged between 50 and 60 years and the same with the numbers of female participants. The researcher randomly recruits until these numbers are reached and then stops.

Quota sampling uses a similar approach to stratified sampling but does not use the process of randomization; the participants are selected as they appear. It is commonly accepted as a form of non-probability sampling and has less credibility than random methods of sampling; however, it does ensure that the sample is as representative as possible as it tries to include each segment of society that possess the characteristic under investigation. Many attributes or stratas can be used, for example age, gender, ethnicity, diagnosis and educational levels.

Cluster sampling or multistage sampling involves the successive random sampling of large units down to smaller ones. It is more economical than other forms of random sampling but equally time-consuming. For example, you may want to know whether introducing curfews for teenagers is effective in reducing crime rates in a specific area so you begin by selecting a town from a selection of towns that use this method, i.e. from a cluster of towns. You then narrow this down to some specific estates or areas from these towns so that you sample a cluster of estates and then narrow this down to sampling individuals drawn from these areas, i.e. clusters of people. This is less representative than a simple random sample as some areas, towns and people are systematically excluded; however, it may be more in depth.

Exercise 3.5

In the following examples consider what type of sampling has been used and if it may be considered representative. The answers are in the Appendix.

Example 1
An experiment aimed to prove that eating oranges improves memory function in people under the age of 45 years.
    The sample consisted of: n = 1000, 825 were women and 175 were men. For each gender 25 per cent were 6–15 years, 16–25, 26–35, 36–45.

Example 2
A survey investigated whether consumers prefer apple-scented soap or vanilla.
    The sample consisted of: n = 1000, 503 were women and 497 were men. 50 per cent were aged between 25 and 40 years and 50 per cent were aged 41–50 years. 100 participants were selected by selecting every tenth person on the list.

Problems with sampling

Accessing, recruiting and retaining the participants is always problematic and many researchers never obtain their sample size. Some samples can be obtained through the use of a sampling frame which lists every potential participant, for example, the use of a telephone directory, a register or from marketing materials. Recruiting minority subjects can be particularly challenging due to language and cultural constraints. Burns and Grove (2006) highlight that studies should be carried out in a timely manner as retaining participants decreases with the length of the study. Inclusion and exclusion criteria that are too stringent can also limit the size of the sample and poorly communicated objectives have also been cited as a barrier to selection.

Sampling bias can be present when some strata of a population are excluded from a study. For example, if an online survey is performed, all of those without internet access are automatically excluded; this impacts the generalizability of the results and a sampling error can occur. Another example could occur through the use of telephone sampling. In order to conduct a successful telephone survey, every person must own a telephone and every telephone number must be available. However, some people do not own phones, some may be out of order, some people are ex-directory and many people only use mobile telephones.

Poor response rates can impact the reliability of research. Small samples reduce the possibility of statistically significant results so quantitative studies rely heavily upon adequate response rates. The lower the response rate, the less likely it is that the sample will be representative of the larger population. Poor response rates have been attributed to: questionnaires that are not written in a persuasive manner, lack of knowledge about the research topic, lack of confidence in the researcher and feeling coerced into complying.

Inclusion and exclusion criteria are used to limit the study population in order to make it manageable and increase the focus of the sample. These criteria set the parameters of the study by identifying who should be included and excluded and why. Strictly limiting the sample also increases the precision of a study, protects any vulnerable members of the population and controls for any factors that could contaminate the research (extraneous variables). For example, when studying a sample of healthcare students the inclusion criteria could consist of: all full-time students on an undergraduate degree programme, all students who have successfully passed at least three modules, all students who have access to home internet services. You may wish to exclude: all part-time students, all those who have learning disabilities, all of those with any current serious illness and all of those who do not have home internet services. Sometimes inclusion and exclusion criteria are governed by ethical principles to protect participants and sometimes by the nature of the research question or hypothesis.

Data collection methods

Quantitative researchers need to collect data that can be analysed statistically and therefore data collection methods need to facilitate this. The data collection method needs to be either suitable for sampling large numbers of people or for measuring cause and effect. The most popular data collection methods tend to be surveys and experiments. Each of these will be discussed in depth.

Surveys: if you want to know something, why not just ask?

Parahoo (1993) is famous for stating that to some people surveys are a necessary nuisance and for others they are just a nuisance. However, they remain the quickest way to collect large amounts of data quickly and are the most popular data collection tool. Most healthcare professionals use the survey method to assess patients so it fits well with current practice; for example, social workers, nurses and health visitors currently use the Unified Assessment tool which is a form of survey as it questions patients about their current bio-psycho-social status. Managers use patient satisfaction surveys to highlight issues relating to high and low quality patient care.

A survey is a method of collecting data by sampling a cross-section of people who may have a viewpoint about a topic or have some characteristics in common. They can be *descriptive* or *inferential*; the type of survey determines the statistical tests that will be applied. Inferential (or explanatory) surveys are used to determine relationships or correlations between factors while descriptive surveys focus on determining the characteristics of a population. The structured questionnaire is the preferred measuring instrument and is defined by Parahoo (2006) as an instrument consisting of a series of questions and/or attitude statements designed to elicit responses which can be measured.

The notion of the questionnaire as an instrument implies, as with most instruments, that some level of skill is needed to utilize it. When designing questionnaires the skill lies in defining the questions to be asked. Surveys are only reliable if:

- you talk to the right number of people;
- you talk to the right type of people;
- you ask the right questions;
- you analyse the data in the right way (this will be covered in depth in Chapter 4).

Each of these criteria will now be discussed.

Talk to the right number of people

To illustrate how to access the right number of people we could consider the following scenario: you want to know how the public are likely to feel about the introduction of healthcare support workers performing some element of your current role.

1   Who would you want to target as your sample?
2   Would you sample all of those who have received some care at some time by a healthcare support worker?
3   Would you sample every patient who has attended for care?
4   Would you use random sampling or non-random sampling?
5   How many people should you sample?

It is difficult to make generalizations from a small sample and they may not be considered reliable. Talking to the right number of people is problematic as questionnaires tend to have the highest non–response rates compared to other forms of data gathering. Burns and Grove (2006) state that a response rate of less than 50 per cent seriously impacts the robustness of the study. Completing a questionnaire requires motivation and interest.

Exercise 3.6

Identify why people may not complete a questionnaire. What features of questionnaires could put people off completing them? How can these barriers be decreased?

One advantage of questionnaires concerns the opportunity to remain anonymous and confidential so that participants can express a critical view without any fear of reprisals. This can encourage participation and honesty; however, the lack of direct contact can also be a barrier.

Talk to the right type of person

Accessing the right type of person can also be problematic as the participants need to be knowledgeable about the topic area – how can this be assured? As many questionnaires are distributed by post, respondents are not assessed in any way; furthermore, there is no opportunity for respondents to validate their responses or ask questions. Understanding the questionnaire and the responses are taken for granted by both parties. This has the potential to impact the reliability and validity of the responses as respondents may be forced to guess the answers. In order to access the right types of person the researcher needs to consider:

- ***The participants' knowledge of the subject area*** as there is no advantage in targeting people who have had no exposure to the topic area; the responses could skew the results. Sometimes talking to the right person involves accessing the views of the most knowledgeable people. The Delphi technique is a form of survey that is used to determine the judgements of experts for the purpose of making decisions or designing policies in health care. A questionnaire with open and closed questions is distributed to a panel that are anonymous to each other. The results are then analysed statistically and if there are any extreme results, a second questionnaire is sent out asking participants to clarify and justify their responses. This procedure is repeated until there is a consensus of opinion. However, achieving a consensus is not always an outcome and often a 'majority rules' notion is applied. Of course, the obvious questions here are: what counts as an expert? Who decides? And is there the potential for researcher bias as the experts are selected?

- **the capacity** of the participants in order to adhere to ethical principles;
- **the homogeneity and heterogeneity** of the sample. These two terms describe the extent to which the sample is the same in its characteristics (homogeneity) or different (heterogeneity). Sometimes a researcher may need a sample to be as similar as possible in order to demonstrate that it is an accurate reflection of normal society and sometimes they may wish the sample to be very different in order to demonstrate that a tool is reliable across multiple types of people.

Ask the right questions

A good questionnaire should be valid and reliable. *Validity* refers to the extent to which the instrument measures the constructs that it is claiming to measure; for example, if the research question is concerned with measuring patients' attitudes about caring, the questionnaire must have sufficient and relevant questions to reflect the nature of caring. This is termed *construct* or *face validity*. One of the problems for questionnaires concerns the types of topics that they are designed to investigate. For example, they are often used to measure constructs such as pain, caring, attitudes, depression, etc. These are terms that rarely have any concrete meaning which raises the question, how can they claim to be valid if the underlying constructs themselves cannot be globally defined? One method of ensuring construct validity is to use the CVI (Content Validity Index) technique. The questionnaire is given to a team of experts who review the items and compare them with other items in other tools in order to confirm their legitimacy. Piloting the questionnaire on a sample prior to the study is also a highly valued way of enhancing validity and reliability.

Reliability

Reliability is concerned with the extent to which the questionnaire can be repeated in order to elicit a similar response or understanding. In order to reduce the element of bias questionnaires should be presented in a consistent manner. Keeping the questions as closed as possible is one strategy used to enhance consistency; however, this can limit the opportunity for truthfulness as the participants can be 'straight-jacketed' into selecting from the choices available rather than expressing their real preference. One concern when designing a questionnaire is how to word the items. The wording of questions can influence respondents to give the desired response rather than an honest one, creating a bias. Questionnaires rely upon accurate and honest reporting so the language should be unambiguous and jargon free. They should be written within the capacity of the least able respondent but assessing this is again problematic when the researcher has no prior contact with the participants. Asking the same standardized questions to every respondent does not presume that understanding has occurred.

Language is culturally embedded in social patterns and decoding the questions and responses is a process of interpretation. One way to widen access is to reduce the amount of wordage by using a scale which involves using an ordered series of categories that are placed along a continuum and awarded a numerical value. Three main types of scales tend to be used in surveys: Likert scales, semantic differential scales and visual analogue scales. Each of these will now be discussed.

Likert scales

These were introduced by Rensis Likert, a sociologist from Michigan in 1932, and tend to be used to measure attitudes. This involves presenting a series of statements about a topic and asking the respondents to indicate the extent to which they agree or disagree. An example could be: you want to know if patients perceive physiotherapists as kind so you design a scale with five response categories, two positive, two negative and one neutral one (see Figure 3.1). This is the norm for most Likert scales.

Exercise 3.7

Can you identify any pros and cons of using this approach?

Semantic differential scales

Instead of using words to measure the variable under investigation a number can be applied. For example, in order to rate the degree of kindness from 1–5,

Category	Strongly agree	Agree	Uncertain	Disagree	Strongly disagree
Physiotherapists always listen to our problems					
Physiotherapists go out of their way to solve our expressed problems					
Physiotherapists always talk to us in a gentle manner					
Physiotherapists always use touch effectively to reduce any chance of pain					

Figure 3.1 Example of a Likert scale.

1 could be very unkind and 5 could be very kind with measures in between. This type of scale is referred to as a semantic differential: semantics refers to words and differential refers to the bipolar nature of the words, i.e. opposites. This type of scale was introduced in 1957 by Osgood, Suci and Tannenbaum and was designed to measure variations of a concept. To enhance the ease of response, data can also be presented visually in the form of a visual analogue scale.

Visual analogue scales

A visual analogue scale is used to measure subjective experience or perceptions such as anxiety, pain or motivation. It consists of a horizontal or vertical line that has extreme limits of a variable. Respondents select a point along the line that best indicates their feelings about the variable under investigation. These scales are particularly useful for people who are challenged in some way in terms of reading and writing as pictorial anchors can be used at either end rather than words and as few words are used they are easily applied to other countries (see Figure 3.2). Furthermore, the visual nature of the scale elicits a quick response, which it could be argued, is more genuine as little thinking time is required.

This section has discussed the type of scales that are used in surveys. Scales are particularly useful when the researcher has no knowledge of the

How kind do you find physiotherapists?

Very kind ← Very unkind

Figure 3.2 An example of a visual analogue scale.

participants and their capacity cannot be assessed. In order to capture the widest audience researchers will often use a variety of scales in any one survey.

To summarize the use of questionnaires, it can be argued that questionnaires have the capacity to capture large amounts of data very quickly; the data can then be analysed statistically by computers in order to reduce the possibility of researcher bias. However, what is gained by the speed of method can be balanced by the loss of substance as data can be superficial and lack the type of depth required for deep understanding. Data from questionnaires is often context free and reveals little about any predisposing historical or social events that may have influenced the response. This chapter will go on to discuss the second most popular method of data collection used in quantitative studies, the experiment.

Experiments

Every day, without realizing it, we experiment in our lives. We make hypotheses about which route will get us to work quicker or which toys will bring pleasure to our children or what type of food will be the most satisfying. In our professional lives we try positioning patients in different postures in order to determine comfort or try a variety of different dressings on a wound until healing occurs. We investigate cause and effect as routinely as we perform many other of our usual customs. We use trial and error knowledge constantly; however, we do not always have the degree of control over some aspects that would allow us to classify these events as true experiments. Three factors are crucial to the good experiment:

- introducing an intervention
- randomization
- control.

Experiments are designed to make something happen in order to evaluate the effectiveness of an intervention. Unlike surveys which look at correlations, experiments are designed to test cause and effect relationships. The aim of the experiment is to ensure that the intervention that you apply is genuinely responsible for the outcome and that it is not just due to chance. Therefore, the researcher tries to control as many aspects of the research process as possible. This includes carefully selecting subjects by randomization, performing pre- and post-tests, using placebos and blinding subjects so that they are unaware of their status in the control group or the experimental group. In healthcare experiments are referred to as clinical trials or randomized control trials and they are highly regarded for their scientific rigour and reliability.

Types of experiments

In healthcare research there tend to be three types of experiment:

The first is *the true experiment*, which is a comparison of two independent groups, a control group and an experimental group treated under different conditions. For example: you want to know if exposing patients to soft music prior to bedtime will increase the amount of time that they spend sleeping. You develop a research hypothesis such as: 'Playing soft music by Mozart for 30 minutes prior to sleep will increase the number of hours spent sleeping'. You randomly select patients and allocate them into two groups. You play some soft music to group 1 – this will be your experimental group as they are receiving some sort of intervention – and you give nothing to group 2, this is the control group. You have controlled who has the intervention and can then record the amount of sleep that each group experienced. You can then accept or reject the hypothesis.

Barbour et al. (2010) wanted to know whether giving 5 mg of intravenous morphine would reduce the number of rigours experienced by patients with malignant melanoma who were receiving a drug called interleukin-2. They performed a randomized control trial (a true experiment) in 23 patients using a control group (n = 9) and an experimental group (n = 14). The results showed that the group who received the morphine had no rigours compared to the group who did not receive morphine.

Repeated measures experimentation is where you have one group of subjects with a particular complaint and you subject them to different conditions. For example, you want to know which emollient from a choice of five will most effectively moisturize very dry skin. So you expose your sample to each of the five emollients in turn and monitor the effects. Can you see any potential problems with this method? For example, how can we be sure that the change is due to one particular emollient and not due to the effects of two that have unexpectedly worked together? This is commonly referred to as a carry-over effect.

Single subject experimentation is used when only one subject is exposed to multiple conditions and is used where it is not possible to find a large sample with the same or similar characteristics or when little is known about the interventions. This method has less reliability than using multiple subjects as the findings cannot be generalized and also has the potential for a carry-over effect. However, it may be considered patient centred as it focuses on the individuality of the patient, a concept central to healthcare principles.

There are two broad categories of experimental designs: *field* and *laboratory*. Field experiments tend to be performed in a natural setting whereas laboratory experiments take place in a controlled, simulated environment. In order to understand the nature of experiments several key terms need to be explored. The first is 'variable'.

Variables

Experiments cannot exist without variables as these are the factors that are either held constant or manipulated in an experiment. A variable is basically something that can be changed or varied, for example temperature, height and weight. In experiments six types of variables are considered: dependent, independent, confounding, extraneous, demographic and environmental. In a good experiment all of the variables should be explicitly defined and clearly articulated. The last four types are often analysed at the end of a study and presented as a table or as limitations of the study. Each types of variable will now be discussed.

Independent variable

This is the cause of the outcome. It is manipulated so is *independent* of any effect. For example, you formulate the hypothesis 'Using patient controlled analgesia will reduce the intensity of post-operative pain'. Here, the independent variable is the use of patient controlled analgesia as we assume that it will cause a reduction in pain intensity. The independent variable is always the intervention that is applied.

Dependent variable

This is the effect or consequence of the independent variable so it depends upon it for any change to occur. It is not manipulated, it is observed and measured. And therefore must have the capability to vary or change. For example, if we return to the hypothesis stated above, the dependent variable is the intensity of post-operative pain as this is the factor that is measured. The change in pain measurement is dependent upon receiving the patient controlled analgesia, hence the outcome depends upon the intervention occurring. Multiple independent and dependent variables can be used in a study but they should be explicitly stated.

Extraneous variable

This is a variable that has the potential to impact the reliability of a study. Extraneous variables can be controlled for at the beginning of the study and could include: height, weight, age, gender of participants. An example of an extraneous variable could be as follows.

You want to determine if exposure to very spicy curry causes an increase in body temperature so you record the temperatures of participants before and after eating a spicy curry. You find that half of the participants have a raised temperature after eating the curry. However, you then discover that half of the sample was sitting next to a hot radiator. Are the results due to the curry or the radiator? In order to establish true cause and effect we would need to control for the effect of the radiator by ensuring that none of the participants were positioned near a radiator.

Confounding variables

A confounding variable is a variable that intervenes outside the purpose of the study that can impact the reliability of the results. Unlike extraneous variables, confounding variables cannot be controlled; examples would include the weather, acts of God, past life experiences, genetic dispositions and age. An example of a confounding variable could be if the radiator were to burst in the example given in the preceding paragraph.

Demographic variables

These are characteristics of the subjects that are collected to describe the sample, for example age, gender, educational level and employment details. In a good experiment participants should be mixed for as many of their characteristics as possible; however, in reality this is problematic as the list could be infinite and new expected variables can possibly present.

Environmental variables

These are extraneous variables bound up in the context of the study that can be controlled in a laboratory, for example: heat, humidity and light. For instance, a researcher may wish to know what temperature is needed to stimulate bacteria growth on a sample of human tissue so he may experiment with different temperatures. He may then wish to know if light has any impact upon bacteria growth and may exposure the skin sample to range of different light sources.

Exercise 3.8

In each of the following sentences identify the independent and dependent variables; there may be more than one type in each. The answers are in the Appendix.

1   Violence on TV causes criminal behaviour.
2   A low fat diet will decrease weight.
3   Men who give women flowers are more likely to get a kiss at the end of the evening.

(continued)

4   Improving education about the correct use of inhaler devices causes an increase in concordance in asthma sufferers.

5   Patients who mobilize directly after surgery experience fewer post-operative complications.

6   Community care clients who keep district nursing notes at home, to which visiting professionals regularly contribute, obtain a more effectively coordinated service.

7   World cup rugby, which is watched by up to 20 million people, is responsible for a sudden upsurge in the national expenditure as more women decide to spend their time shopping online instead of accompanying their men in front of the TV.

Placebo effect

A placebo effect is defined as a perceived improvement or change in condition that is due to a psychological response rather than to any active intervention. Sometimes, it is possible for participants in a study to convince themselves that the new intervention has had a specific effect upon them and this can in turn impact the results of the study. Placebos are one strategy applied to control groups in an attempt to test for any psychological extraneous variables. Another strategy is to blind or double blind the participants. To reduce the element of bias either the participants (single blinding) or both the participants and the researcher (double blinding) are denied knowledge about who has been allocated to the experimental and control groups. Barbour et al. (2010) used a placebo in their experiment into the use of morphine to reduce the incidence of rigours in patients with melanomas and found that the placebo did not influence the incidence of rigours hence there was no obvious placebo effect. The issue with this type of study concerns the ethical principle of equity: is it morally right to offer a drug to some people and deny it to others if you believe that the drug will induce a positive effect?

Quasi-experiment

For ethical or pragmatic reasons it is not always possible to carry out a true experiment. For example, a ward manager may want to know if electronic rostering produces a balanced skill mix compared to traditional rostering. The manager may compare two wards but they are not randomly selected as there may only be one ward that performs electronic rostering, therefore they have to use a convenience sample. This is an appropriate method to use when the researcher wants to cause minimum disruption in a natural setting.

However, as the researcher is unable to control for extraneous variables, they cannot confidently state that the results are due to the intervention, therefore a quasi-experiment does not guarantee the same level of reliability as the true experiment.

To summarize experiments, they can be criticized on several counts: first McEvoy and Richards (2006) claim that experiments tend to focus exclusively on the cause and effect event in isolation from the context in which they occur. They point out that social events cannot be cut off from external influences as effects arise due to the interaction between social structures and human agency. Therefore, the control that is so crucial to experiments is essentially flawed thinking. The second criticism concerns the notion that results can occur naturally with or without the intervention. This is referred to as serendipity, which means making happy discoveries by accident (Sheehan 1986). However, despite the limitations identified experiments are regarded as the highest level of evidence by many researchers due to their high levels of reliability and generalizability.

Summary

The purpose of this chapter is to identify the key components of quantitative research and discuss them in some depth. Two schools of philosophy have been identified that underpin quantitative research; these have been identified as positivism and post-positivism. Positivism has been described as perceiving humans as closed systems that can be objectively observed and measured in order to establish laws and truths. Post-positivism has been described as a later version of positivism with some differences; for example, post-positivists believe that establishing absolute truth is unrealistic and instead explore the plausible rather than the actual. Both schools of thought have their rightful place in the study of health care and it is the extent to which the researcher believes in the notion of objectivity that will direct the stance that is adopted. The process of obtaining data has been discussed and two methods appear to dominate the quantitative paradigm: surveys and experiments. Each has been evaluated for its strengths and weaknesses. The sampling techniques required in both methods have been debated. Several techniques have been discussed but the process of randomization has been identified as the most robust approach as it achieves a high level of reliability. The next chapter will discuss how to analyse the data produced from quantitative research and will enhance your understanding of the quantitative paradigm.

Jargon busting

Make a list of any words in this chapter that you do not understand. Look up their meaning and consider their use in the world of research. You may identify some of the following words and terms:

Bias: A conscious or unconscious prejudice that could impair the results of a study.

Homogeneous: Uniform in nature or of the same kind.

Hypothesis: A statement of prediction about causal factors.

Hypothetico-deductive method: A deductive approach devised by Karl Popper that is used to scientifically test a hypothesis.

Objectivity: Being detached from the research data, being unseen.

Positivism: The philosophy that underpins quantitative research.

Sample: A section of a population who are chosen to be participants in a research study.

Sampling bias: This is the over or under representation of a particular element of a population.

Strata: A segment of a population that have a specific characteristic.

References

Barbour, L., Kosirog-Glowacki, J., Pharm, D., et al. (2010) Evidence for biologic therapy rigour control: placebo-controlled trial in intravenous morphine, in M.M. Kirkpatrick McLaughlin and S. Bulla (eds) (2010) *Real Stories of Nursing Research*. London: Jones and Bartlett Publishers.

Borbasi, S., Jackson, D. and Langford, R.W. (2004) *Navigating the Maze of Nursing Research: An Interactive Learning Adventure*. London: Mosby.

Bowling, A. (2009) *Research Methods in Health: Investigating Health and Health Services*. Maidenhead: Open University Press.

Burns, N. and Grove, S.K. (2006) *The Practice of Nursing Research: Conduct, Critique and Utilization*, 5th edn. St Louis, MO: Elsevier Saunders.

Cheng, C., Studdiford, J.S., Chambers, C.V., Diamond, J.J. and Paynter, N. (2002) The reliability of patient self-reported blood pressures, *Journal of Clinical Hypertension*, 4(4): 259–64.

Coolican, H. (2004) *Research Methods and Statistics in Psychology*. London: Hodder and Stoughton.

Descartes (1637) Cited in: Halverston, W. (1976) *A Concise Introduction to Philosophy*, 3rd edn. New York: Random House.

Gouldner, A. (1991) Cited in M. Hammersly (1999) Sociology, what is it for? A critique of Gouldner, *Sociology Research Online*, 4(3): 1.

Hunter, L. and Leahey, E. (2008) Collaborative research in sociology: trends and contributing factors, *American Sociologist*, 39: 290–306.

LoBiondo-Wood, G. and Haber, J. (2010) *Nursing Research: Methods and Critical Appraisal for Evidence Based Practice*. Missouri: Mosby Elsevier.

McEvoy, P. and Richards, D. (2006) A critical realist rationale for using a combination of quantitative and qualitative methods, *Journal of Research in Nursing*, 11(1): 66–78.

Mitroff, I. (1974) Cited in: Coolican, H. (2004) *Research methods and statistics in psychology*. London: Hodder and Stoughton.

Mulhall, M. and Le May, A. (1999) *Nursing Research: Dissemination and Implementation*. London: Churchill Livingstone.

Parahoo, K. (1993) Questionnaires: use, value and limitations. *Nurse Researcher*, 1(2): 4–15.

Parahoo, K. (2006) *Nursing Research: Principles, Processes and Issues*. Basingstoke: Palgrave Macmillan.

Polit, D.F. and Beck, C.T. (2010) *Nursing Research: Appraising Evidence for Nursing Practice*, 7th edn. Philadelphia, PA: Lippincott, Williams and Wilkins.

Popper, K.R. (1959) *The Logic of Scientific Discovery*. London: Hutchinson.

Rawl, S.M., Given, B.A. and Given, C.W. (2002) Intervention to improve psychological functioning, *Oncology Nursing Forum*, 29: 967–75.

Sheehan, J. (1986) Aspects of research methodology, *Nurse Education Today*, 6: 193–203.

4 Analysis of quantitative data

Introduction

> Quantitative data would be chaos without statistics, which allow for summarization, organization, interpretation and communication.
>
> (Shara 2010: 25)

To define statistics as fun may be optimistic and from personal experience, many students tremble at the thought of statistics; however, once fear is faced, like all fears, it can be overcome. There really is no need to panic as due to computer aided packages, you don't even need to do sums! In order to appreciate and critique evidence you just need to understand the rules. This chapter will enhance your understanding of statistical tests and hopefully help to alleviate some of the anxiety. The aim of this chapter is not to prepare you to become a statistician, it is to enable you to engage with data in order to recognize when appropriate and inappropriate tests have been applied to research findings. You cannot be critical of research if you do not understand how the findings have been analysed.

In healthcare research all statistical data is counted, ordered and sorted. In principle this sounds simple. Shara (2010) highlights that statistics are simply tools that enable us to make sense of research data in a way that can be applied to practice; for example, without statistics we would have no disease rates to direct our work and no idea which strategies work and which ones don't. As with most research principles, statistics are an integral part of daily life. For example, we use statistics to calculate our shopping, estimate mileage and we could not use money without some idea of statistics, hence it is not an alien concept. Numbers are more precise than words and are easier to visualize. For example, it is easier to visualize a person who weighs 120 kilograms than to say a very big person as big can mean many things.

Learning objectives

At the end of this chapter you will be able to:

- differentiate between descriptive and inferential statistics;
- demonstrate an understanding of the common terms used in statistical analysis;
- distinguish between different types of data;
- identify when to use parametric and non-parametric tests.

Types of statistics

Different types of studies require different types of statistics but these can be easy to remember if you learn the terms. Two types of statistics are used in quantitative research: descriptive and inferential. If a study seeks to explore the characteristics of a population descriptive statistics are used, but if the researcher wishes to look at relationships where inferences need to be made about the impact of variables, inferential statistics would be used.

Descriptive statistics

These describe the characteristics of the sample and are concerned with the extent to which a 'normal' homogenous sample has been obtained. They define the parameters of the population by identifying the extremes which then helps to determine the norm. The researcher needs to be confident that the results of the study are due to the intervention applied and not due to an abnormal sample. How can a researcher ever be truly sure that the sample is normal? Is it possible to ever achieve a normal sample? It is unreasonable to expect a sample to be exactly the same as the general population; however, we can expect it to be reasonably close provided that the sample is a large enough one and is not disproportionally atypical. Researchers accept that there is always the potential for error in a sample but it is the degree of error that signifies whether the results are significant or not. A figure of 5 per cent error is acceptable for the majority of researchers; hence the researcher needs to be assured that 95 per cent of the sample may be considered homogenous (the same). This is termed the *confidence interval*. In other words for every 100 people in the sample, no more than five can be 'strange'.

The 5 per cent degree of error can also be applied if we consider the intervention as the researcher also wants to be 95 per cent confident that the results are due to the intervention rather than due to chance. If we cannot be confident that the results are due to the intervention, the results are deemed non-significant and the hypothesis is rejected. If we can be 95 per cent certain that the results are due to the intervention we can state that the results are significant and we can accept the hypothesis.

The term *probability* is used to predict the likelihood of an event happening and is measured as a decimal rather than as a percentage. So while a confidence interval would be written as 95 per cent, probability would be written as 0.05. The probability of an outcome happening varies from zero to one. Both measures look for a level of less than 5 per cent to prevent an error from occurring. The smaller the p value, the less likely that the results have occurred by chance. If the p value is less than 0.05 we can state that the results are significant (due to the intervention) and would accept the hypothesis. This would be written as $p < 0.05$. The larger the sample size, the less the potential for error. Sometimes the researcher may want a smaller potential for sample error, for example in a drug trial where there may be the potential for side effects, the researcher may want a probability of $p < 0.005$ which would mean that only five people out of 1000 would be acceptable.

Exercise 4.1

Which of these levels would be accepted as significant? The answers are in the Appendix.

1   a probability of 0.005
2   a probability of 0.23
3   a probability of 0.89
4   a probability of 0.1
5   a confidence interval of 98 per cent
6   a confidence interval of 73 per cent

Standard deviation

The extent to which a sample deviates from the norm is measured through the use of *standard deviation* and the results are visually communicated through the use of a distribution curve. This measures the degree of spread. Figures are collected from a group; for example, if a group of students completed an assignment and achieved grades from A to E the number of students who achieved each grade would be calculated and plotted on the graph. In a normal group, whatever the intervention applied, most of the results tend to cluster around the middle. For example, the majority of students tend to achieve C grades and fewer students achieve the grades on either side (see Figure 4.1). Therefore, the graph demonstrates higher ranges in the centre which equates to the average scores and the levels get lower on each side of the middle. Two

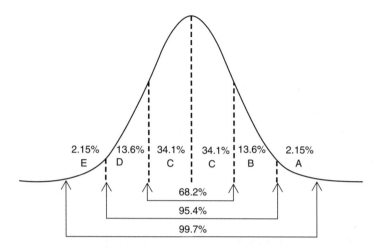

Figure 4.1 Gaussian curve.

thirds (64 per cent) of the results will lie within + or − 1 standard deviation from the average, 95 per cent of the results will lie within 2 standard deviations from the average and 99 per cent will be within 3 standard deviations from the average. Hence the higher the standard deviation, the more spread out the results are and the more the sample is different from the norm. We can see that a bell-shaped curve is produced; this is referred to as a Gaussian curve, named after Carl Frederick Gaussian, a famous mathematician.

If the majority of the sample achieved A grades or E grades the distribution of the results would look different; for example, see the curve in Figure 4.2.

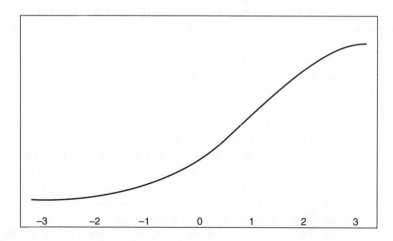

Figure 4.2 An abnormal distribution curve.

We can see that the majority of the scores are towards the +3 range which demonstrates that the majority of students scored highly. This could indicate that this particular sample are cleverer than the average cohort of students or it could hint that they have received an intervention that other students have not received such as extra tutorials. If a Gaussian curve is produced the researcher can be confident that the sample is 'a standard or normal sample' and the researcher can quickly see the extent to which the extremes deviate from the centre. Therefore the standard deviation would be low. However, in Figure 4.2 we can see that at least two or three of the group have achieved higher than average scores and have a higher standard deviation. The further the score is from zero, the higher the standard deviation, hence, the more abnormal the sample or the higher the probability that the result is due to chance.

Another example could be that a midwife wishes to explore the average weight of 20–30-year-old women in her pre-natal clinic. Through statistical knowledge it is already known that the average woman aged between 20 and 30 years weighs 55 kg and the standard deviation is 5.8. This means that two-thirds of the women weigh between 49.2–60.8 kg. These figures describe the parameters of the population, so we know what the average women weigh. The midwife then has a sample of 200 women aged between 20 and 30 years and the average weight is 53.7 kg. It is within the normal distribution of between 49.2 and 60.8 so the sample is considered to be from a normal distribution of women.

Four measurements can be used to describe the sample: frequency, central tendency, measures of spread and measures of shape.

Frequency measures the number of times that a variable occurs, looks for commonalities and observes where variables are grouped. We can also establish the range by identifying the highest and lowest figures. In health care frequency can be used to measure the prevalence of diseases, the incidence of patient complaints or the rate of sickness.

Central tendency describes how the sample's results are clustered together or spread apart. Three values are used to determine the central tendency of data; these are: the mean, median and mode.

- The *mean* refers to the average of all the given scores and is visualized as the central part of the Gaussian curve. This is calculated by adding together all of the responses and dividing it by the number of participants. The mean is vitally important as if we do not know the average measurement of a variable we cannot define the parameters of populations. Without the mean scores we could not calculate the central tendency or the standard deviation.
- The *median* refers to the middle value in a distribution of numbers and this is calculated by ranking the data in order from lowest to

highest and then selecting the value that appears in the middle. If there is an even number of values, the two middle numbers are added together and divided by two.

- The *mode* refers to the most common value.

Why might these values be relevant for health care? Imagine that you want to know if sickness rates have increased or decreased in your clinical area in the last month. You will want to know first the extremes, i.e. the least number of days spent off sick and the most number of days so that you can calculate what is acceptable (this is defining the parameters of the population). You will need to know the average number of staff who had time off work for sickness (the mean) in order to compare this with other units and previous rates. You will need to know the median number in order to establish the norm and the extent to which your staff deviate from it and you will need to calculate the mode to establish what the most commonly occurring illnesses are.

Exercise 4.2

Calculate the mean, median and mode from the following set of statistics. The answers are in the Appendix.

2, 3, 3, 3, 8, 4, 5, 9, 7, 4, 5, 9, 7, 3.

Levels of data

The type of statistical test that should be applied is also determined by the level of measurement. There are four levels of data used.

Interval data describes data that has intervals between each measurement. The distance between each measurement is the same; for example, blood pressure varies by a measurement of 1 between each scale and 2 is twice as much as 1. Other examples include the measurement of temperature, depression ratings, intelligence scores or risk assessment scales. Interval data is very easy to use to establish the parameters of a population as the mean, median and mode can be established quickly and plotted onto a graph to establish variations and patterns. Interval data is used where there is no zero point; for example, it is not possible to have no blood pressure or no temperature. However, the type of measurements that may be classified as interval may be debated; for example, some health professionals would argue that it is not possible to have zero depression as a very low score could indicate that a person feels sad on some occasions. Tools are always open to interpretation.

Ratio data meets the same criteria as interval data in that the units of measurement are an equal distance apart but there is an absolute zero. An example could be income as it is possible to have zero income. Put simply, interval and ratio data are nothing more than simple counting and contain the type of data that could be used in visual analogue scales such as pain scales.

Ordinal data has no mathematical scale but has an order. For example, social class could be used to demonstrate that there are five classes and they rank from highest to lowest but social class three is not three times more than social class one so the intervals between the classes are not the same. Another example could be to rank the heights of a cohort of students. The students could be ranked from tallest to smallest, the smallest would receive a rank of 1 and the tallest receives a rank of 20; however, the tallest student is not 20 times taller than the smallest one. This type of data would often appear in Likert type scales.

Nominal data The term nominal is defined as something that exists in name only, which implies that there is no actual level of measurement as with ratio or interval data. In nominal data there are no mathematical relationships as people are grouped according to a characteristic that they may possess. For example, people may be grouped according to their eye colour, gender, nationality or occupation. The frequency of each category is then measured.

Exercise 4.3

Identify whether these sets of data below are ratio, interval, ordinal or nominal and consider why they meet each classification. The answers are in the Appendix.

1   The number of males and females in a primary school
2   A depression rating scale
3   A pain scale
4   The number of people from each region of the UK who voted for a labour government
5   Money in pence
6   An intelligence rating scale
7   The number of children in a swimming club who received gold, silver and bronze awards
8   Weight measurements from a cohort of ladies in a slimming club
9   A patient satisfaction survey.

Parametric and non-parametric tests

Another consideration in deciding upon the most appropriate test is the choice between a *parametric* or *non-parametric test*. The test depends upon whether the parameters of the population are known. The term *parameter*

refers to the least measurement, average measurement and the highest measurement of the variable under investigation. Sometimes these figures are
known and a Gaussian curve can be observed. As the parameters can be known
we use parametric tests for these kinds of data. If the parameters of the population are not known or are skewed in some way we use non-parametric tests.
Ratio and interval data use parametric tests and ordinal and nominal data use
non-parametric tests (see Figure 4.3). In reality we can never actually know
the true parameters of any population as we cannot measure every person,
therefore any figures represent a best guess.

Exercise 4.4

To test your understanding of descriptive statistics let's play a game called 'find
me'. A number of clues are given on the right-hand side; try to find the answer
that correctly corresponds to the clue. For example, if you think that clue 1
matches J, write 1J. The answers are provided in the Appendix.

Clue	Answer
1 I am data with an absolute zero and equal units of measurement	A Inferential statistics
2 I am a curve	B Range
3 I aim for 95 per cent	
4 I am the spread between the least score and the highest score	C Ordinal data
5 I am data with equal measures but no absolute zero	D Mode
	E Ratio
6 I am data that has no mathematical scale but has an order	F Descriptive statistics
7 I am the most common figure	G Confidence interval
8 I am a measurement of spread, I look at whether data is clustered or spread out	H Probability
9 I am measured as a decimal and need a large sample	I Central tendency
10 I am a type of statistic that examines correlations about variables	J Interval data
11 I measure the characteristics of a population	K Gaussian

Inferential statistics

We have discussed descriptive statistics and have concluded that there are
multiple ways to measure data. Descriptive statistics refer to the sample

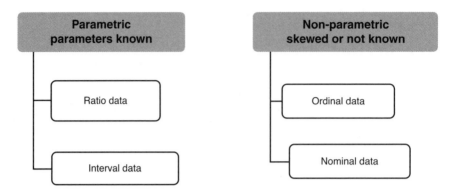

Figure 4.3 Levels of data.

whereas inferential statistics can be used to satisfy inquisitive minds as they seek to measure correlations between variables. Hence they are used to investigate cause and effect and make inferences from the sample that can be applied to the general population. Inferential statistics require three things: two variables, some data and a test. The kinds of conclusions that can be meaningfully drawn from a set of data are dependent upon the right test being applied. The type of test applied depends upon whether the data is parametric (the parameters of the population are known, i.e. they form a normal distribution curve) or non-parametric (the parameters of the population are not known); so how do we know this information? Any new topic where little data exists will always be non-parametric, i.e. a new disease, as we may not have reliable data to confirm the mean, median and mode. As stated, parametric data is usually ratio or interval and non-parametric data is usually ordinal or nominal. The first thing that we need to do is to plot the data on a graph; if the data forms a normal distribution curve it is parametric, if it is skewed it needs a non-parametric test.

Testing samples

A second consideration when determining the test to be applied is the number of variables under investigation and the number of samples that are being compared. For example, if you were investigating correlations between different clinical areas, i.e. job satisfaction between a medical unit and a surgical unit, the results from two independent samples are being compared. The data would be either ratio or interval, depending upon whether there is agreement regarding an absolute absence of satisfaction, so a parametric test called a *t test* would be applied. A t test tests the difference between the means of two independent samples. If more than two samples are used (for example, we wanted to compare satisfaction levels of medical, surgical and mental health nurses) an *ANOVA* (this stands for analysis of variance) test would be used which analyses the variance between the units. If ordinal or nominal level data (non-parametric data) from two samples were being compared, the Mann-Whitney test would be applied if the samples were unrelated, i.e. surgical and medical nurses, or the Wilcoxon test would be applied if the samples were related, i.e. two groups from the same unit. If a small group using nominal level data is used a test called the Fisher Exact test is used.

Testing variables

The ANOVA test is also applied when testing variables as well as referring to samples, for example, if you wanted to know whether obesity is linked to reduced life expectancy and depression. Obesity is measured in BMI which has no absolute zero but has measures in intervals, therefore it is interval data. Life expectancy is measured in years which also has intervals but has an absolute zero so is ratio data. Data exists about the normal distribution of weight and life expectancy in the general population so the parameters are known. Both of these data are parametric so require a parametric test. As there are two dependent variables being investigated the test required would be a two-way ANOVA. If three dependent variables were being studied we would use a three-way ANOVA. If you wanted to measure satisfaction with a new intervention, you could use ordinal data through the use of a semantic differential or Likert scale. Data from the general population may not be available as the intervention has not been applied to them so the parameters are not known, therefore a non-parametric test would be applied. If ordinal or nominal level data (non-parametric) are used the tests that would be applied would be either Kruskal-Wallis if one intervention is applied or the Friedman test if multiple interventions are applied or repeated.

The discussion so far can be summarized as in Table 4.1.

Table 4.1 Statistical tests

Parametric data Ratio/interval	*Test*	*Non-parametric data* Ordinal/nominal	*Test*
1 sample	t test	Related samples	Wilcoxon
2 samples or more	ANOVA	Non-related samples	Mann-Whitney
		Small sample using nominal level data	Fisher Exact
2 or more variables	ANOVA	1 intervention	Kruskal-Wallis
		Multiple interventions	Friedman

Testing for correlations between variables

To test for correlations or relationships between variables a *correlation coefficient* is used; again the clue is in the name. For example, you may want to study the relationship between pressure ulcers and inactivity. The significance of the correlation increases with the sample size, therefore in order to be statistically significant the sample needs to be sufficiently large. If parametric data is used Pearson's correlation coefficient is used and if the data is non-parametric Spearman's correlation coefficient is used. In order to test the significance of change (before and after) a test called the McNemar test can be applied to ordinal or nominal level data.

Measuring frequency

Chi square (written as X^2) is used to measure whether two variables are independent or related. It tests the frequency of observed data and compares the actual with the expected and is used when measuring nominal level data. For example, it is used to test whether the proportions in all categories are the same. So if we wanted to test whether more men or more women suffer from pressure ulcers, we could have a null hypothesis that there will be no difference in the rates of pressure ulcers between men and women (this would be the expected value). We then obtain the numbers of men and women who are classified as having pressure ulcers and compare the observed result with the expected result. We can then determine if gender is or is not related to the incidence of pressure ulcers and either accept or reject the null hypothesis. If the relationship between two variables is tested the Chi 2×2 test is used. We can now add to the table that was presented earlier (see Table 4.2).

Type 1 and 2 errors

Two types of error can occur in research. *A type 1 error* occurs when the null hypothesis is rejected when it is actually true. This means that a statistical test incorrectly finds a significant result where one does not actually exist. The

Table 4.2 Testing correlations and frequency

Parametric data	Test	Non-parametric data	Test
To test correlations	Pearson's correlation coefficient	Tests correlations	Spearman's correlation coefficient
		Measures change	McNemar
		Frequency	Chi square
		Frequency of 2 variables	Chi square 2×2

presence of a type 1 error is detected according to the level of significance which is specified at the design stage in the form of a p value (probability was discussed earlier in this chapter). The level of significance is set at either 0.5 or 0.01 which means that there is a 5 per cent or 1 per cent acceptability of error. Obviously a level of 0.01 will allow for less error as it infers that the results in only 1 person out of every 100 people can be 'odd'.

A *type ll error* is said to occur when the null hypothesis is not rejected when there is an actual difference between the study samples. Sometimes the difference is negligible and does not impact the potential delivery of care; conversely, the error could be very significant and could be detrimental to patient care such as in a drug trial. The error is usually attributed to either a small sample size or crude instrumentation that is not sensitive enough to detect changes. A type ll error can be minimized through the use of power analysis which detects whether the sample is sufficient enough to respond to the variable under investigation. If the power is too low, a larger sample will be required or the study is not worthwhile as the results will not be statistically significant. A measurement of .80 is required for a study to be worthwhile. The power analysis should always be reported in any study that fails to reject the null hypothesis in order to demonstrate rigour within the study. Power analysis can be calculated by using a program called PASS (Power Analysis and Sample Size) that is found in the computer aided package NCSS (Number Crunching Statistical System) or through the use of SPSS (Statistical Packages for Social Sciences).

Computer aided packages

Lowry (2010) points out that computers are marvellous devices that, if applied correctly, can crunch numbers and process information with astonishing speed and accuracy but stresses that regardless of its potential speed, the output can only be as sensible as the data that you input. He states: 'If nonsensical garbage is what you put in, then nonsensical garbage is all that will come out. It will be thoroughly processed nonsense. It might even seem elegant and profound. But it is nonsense all the same' (Lowry 2010).

This argument applies to the study of statistics: if the research process is flawed in any way, the results will be meaningless. Meaningful statistical results are reliant upon the data that has been fed into the computer. Regardless of whether the data is skewed or accurate, the computer will crank out results. Therefore, computer aided results should be viewed with a critical eye and not accepted as truth. Software packages can only do what you ask of them so you need an understanding of the tests that underpin them in order to make sense of the results.

The most popular statistical software for health care is *Statistical Software for the Social Sciences (SPSS)*. SPSS was developed in the 1960s and has undergone numerous updates to remain current and is perhaps the package that is most compatible with home PCs. The main advantage of using a package such as SPSS is the speed at which it can analyse the data. SPSS can be used to test whether data is skewed through using the Skewness statistical package; this will produce a histogram in order to plot the distribution of scores. Again, this result is vulnerable to the number of participants in the sample. SPSS comes with a simple manual for the novice researcher.

Another popular package is *Minitab* which was developed in 1972 in the USA. It is easy to use and has a very professional appearance. Although this is expensive to purchase, students can download a reduced and cheaper version that is suitable for their needs. Minitab is useful for health professionals with an interest in quality improvement as it has an e-learning package called *Quality Trainer* that teaches statistics within the context of clinical governance. Another popular computer package useful for health care is *Statistical Analysis System* (SAS) which is particularly good for report writing, graphics and project management.

Maag (2006) refers to modern students as 'Millennial learners' or digital natives claiming that they have been raised in a media-rich environment and live in a technocratic world where they interact with technology habitually. While this may be true to applications such as internet or Facebook, few modern students have used computer technology to analyse statistics, therefore some packages have been developed specifically for students. *Data Desk* provides fast and easy to use graphics that allow students to look for patterns and relationships and is especially useful for data acquired from surveys and experiments. While it is not free, Data Desk does have three levels of reduced purchase rates for students. There are some free online programmes that students can download such as *Stat Crunch*. Stat Crunch is an entirely web based statistical package that is specifically aimed towards a student audience. Its strengths lie in its simplicity, ease of access and ease of use. As it is web based, it can be accessed anywhere that has internet access, the results are automatically saved to the user's account and it comes with online tutorials.

Summary

This chapter has perhaps been one of the more complex chapters to comprehend as many authors argue that some healthcare professionals, particularly nurses, midwives and allied professionals are uncomfortable with statistical techniques (Ratcliffe 1998). Two types of statistics have been discussed throughout this chapter:

- Descriptive statistics are useful in determining the parameters of populations and describe the characteristics of samples. They tend to use interval and ratio data. The types of tests that apply to parametric data have been discussed and presented in a table. The relevance of descriptive statistics for health care has been briefly discussed; for example, disease rates, obesity rates and demographic statistics are reliant upon parametric data. Even the very basic assessment procedures require some parametric data such as height, weight, blood pressure and blood levels.

- Inferential statistics have been identified as those that measure relationships between variables; they use non-parametric tests and apply to ordinal and nominal levels of data.

The right test for the right data has been tabulated according to whether the data meets the criteria for parametric or non-parametric testing. Identifying the most appropriate test can only be learned through practice. Students often ask 'how do you get to know which test is the right one?' As with many things in life, some things just 'are as they are' and you have to accept that certain data requires a certain test. Throughout this chapter I have tried to show that understanding can often be acquired by thinking about the language that is used. Students have no reason to fear statistics as they are no more than numbers.

Reflective activity

Collect some data from your class cohort or from colleagues whom you work with; for example, you could collate the ages, genders, heights, blood pressures or weights of all of your colleagues. Access one of the computer aided packages discussed within this chapter and play with the data. The results do not have to be precise but this activity will increase your confidence in accessing and interpreting data.

Jargon busting

Make a list of any words in this chapter that you do not understand. Look up their meaning and consider their use in the world of research. You may identify some of the following words and terms:

Central tendency: The extent to which the results are clustered around the centre or are spread out.

Confidence interval: The interval that is set at the beginning of a study that decides what degree of error is acceptable, i.e. the amount of confidence that the researcher has in the accuracy of the results.

Descriptive statistics: Statistics used to describe the characteristics of a sample.

Frequency: The number of times that a variable occurs.

Homogenous sample: The extent to which a sample is similar or the same.

Inferential statistics: Statistics that measure relationships or correlations between variables, i.e. cause and effect.

Interval data: Data that has equal intervals of measurement with no zero.

Mean: The average of all the given scores.

Median: The middle value in a group of numbers.

Mode: The most commonly occurring number.

Nominal data: Data that has no order or ranking but describes characteristics held by a group.

Non-parametric data: Data obtained when the parameters of the population are unknown.

Non-significant: The results obtained may be due to chance or error and therefore the hypothesis may not be accepted.

Ordinal data: Data that has an order but not of equal proportions.

Parametric data: Data obtained when the parameters of the population are known.

Probability: The likelihood of an event happening or that the outcome is due to the intervention.

Ratio data: Data that has equal units of measurement and an absolute zero.

Significant: The extent to which the result can be viewed as reliable and valid which allows the hypothesis to be accepted.

Standard deviation: The extent to which the results obtained from the sample deviate from the norm.

References

Lowry, R. (2010) *Principles of measurement.* http://faculty.vassar.edu/lowry/ch1pt1.html (accessed 17 September 2010).

Maag, M.O. (2006) Podcasting and MP3 players: emerging educational technologies. Computing, *Informatics Nurse*, 24(1), 9–12.

Ratcliffe, P. (1998) Using the new statistics in nursing research, *Journal of Advanced Nursing*, 27: 132–9.

Shara, N.M. (2010) Statistical analysis is a healthcare tool. Book chapter in: Kirkpatrick McLaughlin, M. and Bulla, S. *Real Stories of Nursing Research*. London: Jones and Barlett Publishers. Chapter 5, pp. 25–30.

5 Qualitative research

Introduction

In chapters 3 and 4 we focused on understanding the nature of quantitative research and described some of the key functions it serves such as looking for patterns, identifying trends and correlations and establishing cause and effect. In quantitative research large samples are required to enhance the reliability of the results, random sampling techniques are preferred to minimize the potential for bias and the researcher adopts an objective, detached stance.

This chapter will explore the qualitative paradigm of research. Qualitative research essentially explores why and how people behave as they do. It seeks to establish intentions, motivations and experiences. Whereas quantitative research seeks to predict behaviour, qualitative research tries to understand it. In contrast to the very scientific nature of positivism, qualitative research will be described as interactive, subjective and contextual.

Example

If we consider the issue of obesity, the quantitative researcher may want to establish how many people in the UK may be defined as obese in order to predict the potential problems for future health care or may want to establish which strategies work for obese clients in order to rationalize the appropriate use of resources. In contrast, the qualitative researcher may wish to explore what being obese means for people in terms of how they are able to function, how it impacts their self-esteem and their decision-making processes, and use these findings to improve care strategies. This type of data cannot be acquired through experimentation or objective surveys, because the researchers need to enter the participant's world and interact with them. Laverty (2003) highlights that since the mid-1980s quantitative research has been unable to answer many of the questions crucial to healthcare research and qualitative research has grown in popularity. This chapter will explore the philosophical underpinnings of qualitative research, the sampling processes used and the different methods used to acquire data.

Learning outcomes

At the end of this chapter you will be able to:

- describe the philosophical underpinnings of qualitative research;
- identify the key features of qualitative research;
- demonstrate an awareness of sampling techniques used in qualitative research;
- compare and contrast the range of data collection methods used to gather qualitative data.

Philosophical underpinnings

Three terms are usually used to describe qualitative research: interpretivism constructivism and naturalism. Each of these three notions will be explored in this section.

Interpretivism

Qualitative research is grounded in interpretive philosophy as it is concerned with how the social world is interpreted, understood and experienced. Interpretivism is underpinned by two assumptions: first that multiple valid realities exist and second that subjectivity is the key to understanding. These two assumptions will be discussed here.

The notion of multiple realities

Interpretivists assert that human experience is understood according to how each individual interprets it and that this is impacted by previous experiences and perceptions. Therefore this makes humans very knowledgeable and worthy of investigation. Unlike positivists who seek to establish truth in the world, interpretivists argue that absolute truth does not exist as we all interpret phenomena differently. Therefore there are multiple realities and each one is valid and truthful. Just because one person perceives or experiences an event in a certain way does not negate the different experience of another person. We cannot climb inside the experience of another person, and therefore someone else's experience has to be regarded as honest. As the experience is individual to that person, the honesty of the interpretation cannot be challenged and is regarded as having high internal validity. Laverty (2003) refers to internal validity as a faithful description of the lived experience.

Subjectivity

Interpretivists believe that humans cannot achieve complete objectivity as they exist in and experience the world around them, using their senses to subjectively make sense of phenomena. Qualitative researchers seek to make connections between events, perceptions and actions by *listening* to descriptions or narratives through interviews, by *watching* in the field through ethnography or *interpreting* through the reading of case studies and histories. In these ways the researcher gets close to the research and interacts with both the participants and the data in order to describe it as closely as possible to how participants feel and live it. Interpretivism fits well with health care as caring for people requires an in-depth understanding of patient's beliefs, cultural norms and behaviours. In order to care and cure we need to interact with patients. For example, we cannot assess a patient effectively without listening to their histories and observing their presentation. We basically collect data from patients through the assessment process, analyse the data and produce plans of care.

Whereas quantitative research relies upon objectivity, qualitative research is dependent upon subjectivity. Subjectivity is accepted as essential to both the participant and to the researcher: it is relevant to the participant as it is their personal world that is being explored and it is crucial to the researcher as the researcher is using their own subjectivity to interpret the data given by the participant. In this way the researcher has to be regarded as a research instrument as they are an integral part of the process. In quantitative research, the presence of the researcher is considered a bias but in qualitative research the researcher is viewed as natural and necessary to the process. The researcher's personality, communication skills and influence are crucial to promoting the levels of interaction and trust that are required in order to obtain rich data.

Constructivism

Constructivists believe that reality is constructed by subjectively engaging with objects within the world. The difference between interpretivists and constructivists lies in their perceptions of how phenomena occur. Interpretivists believe that phenomena occur naturally and we just uncover them, whereas constructivists believe that we construct reality incrementally through experience, language and concepts. Constructivists believe that understanding is organized according to clusters of ideas that come together to form a theory to 'see how things make sense'.

For example, in order to understand how an obese person perceives their self-image the researcher has to understand how the person gained weight in the first place. This may involve gaining knowledge of their family history, norms and beliefs and their genetic makeup, exploring their knowledge of nutrition and investigating their social practices such as occupation, exercise, hobbies and limitations. The researcher builds up a picture of the reality until it makes sense to them. In this way the researcher is able to view the depth and complexity of the participant's experience. This is very relevant to health care as we have to construct profiles of patients/clients in order to understand their needs; we need to ascertain what led to their ill health before we can begin to create change or cure for them.

Naturalism

Unlike quantitative research which tends to detach people from their contexts, qualitative research seeks to study people in their natural settings in order to develop a deep understanding of their social reality. Naturalists believe that researchers cannot understand real life if people are examined from outside of their natural settings as context and culture are reduced. This impacts the ability to understand the participants holistically. Data is contextually sensitive and when gathered, attention is spent on preserving the cultural and social context as much as possible. Naturalists believe that meaning is only relevant within a given setting or context and that this meaning will change as the setting changes. This notion contrasts with interpretivism as interpretivist theory believes that the person is central whereas naturalism believes that the setting is central.

Types of qualitative research

Six approaches to qualitative research are used in healthcare research:

1   phenomenology
2   grounded theory
3   ethnography
4   narrative research
5   case studies
6   action research.

Although each approach claims to be qualitative they each differ in their philosophical standpoint and their approach to data gathering and analysis.

Each approach will be discussed in the context of its relevance to health care.

Phenomenology

Phenomenology is concerned with understanding the essence of lived experiences of people and the meanings that people attach to these experiences. Not only is the world experienced differently by each person but their concerns and stressors are qualitatively unique. Phenomenologists believe in the notion of multiple realities. If we refer back to the three philosophical underpinnings of qualitative research we can see that phenomenology tends to be interpretivist and constructivist as we interpret the participant's world through dialogue and relate this to additional social knowledge in order to make sense of it. This is particularly important in order to investigate perceptions of experiences such as suffering chronic pain, trying to understand the meaning of caring, evaluating levels of satisfaction with services, understanding the experience of domestic violence or assessing quality of life. For example, Innes (1998) used phenomenology to explore the experience of stress in radiology students and Coombs et al. (2003) used it to explore the experiences and perceptions of radiologists when exploring the NHS as an employer.

Exercise 5.1

Can you think of a topic that could be investigated using phenomenology in your clinical area?

What sort of research questions would you generate?

How would answering these questions enhance the delivery of care for your clients/patients?

Phenomenology is both a philosophy and a research method. It is a philosophy because it is underpinned by a particular standpoint which directs how data should be gathered and interpreted and it is a research method because it has a strict and rigorous systematic process that must be adhered to. The process is inductive and can be characterized as in the flow chart seen in Figure 5.1.

There are two dominant philosophical schools of thought regarding what counts as true phenomenology namely: *descriptive phenomenology* which is attributed to Edmund Husserl (1859–1938) and *hermeneutic phenomenology* used by Martin Heidegger (1889–1976). Both styles accept that phenomenology is concerned with constructing the meaning of human experience through intensive dialogue with the person who has lived the experience and secondly

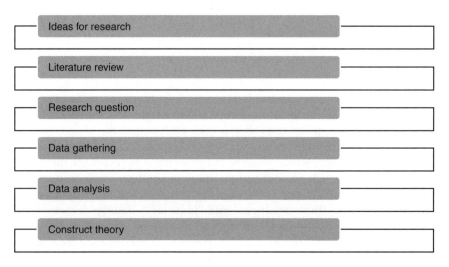

Figure 5.1   The phenomenological process.

that the experience is impacted by the individual senses and the social context. Hence, phenomenology asks the question 'what is the essence of *that experience* for *that person?*' However, Husserl and Heidegger disagree regarding the position of the researcher. Husserl argues that the researcher has the potential to contaminate or bias the research through their personal interpretations of the world and should therefore 'bracket' these understandings. Bracketing involves acknowledging one's preconceived ideas and holding them in abeyance. In other words the researcher has to try to un-know what they already know about the world. Alternatively, Heidegger argues that bracketing is unrealistic and accepts that the researcher will always apply their interpretation to the participant's narrative as the researcher exists in the world and is an integral part of the research process.

Exercise 5.2

Consider the following questions:

1   *Is it possible to bracket what you already know?*
    Consider the issue of caring. You have probably experienced some different types of caring during your lifetime. Write down what you understand by the term caring and reflect upon some of your experiences of receiving and giving care. Now put what you have written to one side and ask a colleague what they understand about caring. Write down your interpretation of your colleague's perception of caring. Was your colleague's interpretation very

different to your own or was it similar? Was it possible to interpret their dialogue without applying any of your own understandings?

2   *What is the researcher's level of insight into the phenomena described? Can they really understand it in the same way as the participant?*
Did your colleague describe any experiences, words or images that you could not relate to? If so, were they less meaningful to you than the experiences or words that you recognized?

Imagine that you are sitting in an open area and an alien lands next to you. The alien asks you to describe your world to him. You begin to tell the alien about television, computers and cars. The alien lives in a soft world with no corners or hard surfaces; can you really expect the alien to construct an image of a computer when he has no concept of 'hard'? Thinking deeply about these questions will help you to critically consider the strengths and weaknesses of each phenomenological approach.

The two phenomenological approaches can be summarized as in Figure 5.2.

Grounded theory

The term grounded theory was coined in 1967 by social scientists Glaser and Strauss and is used to examine the social and psychological structures that

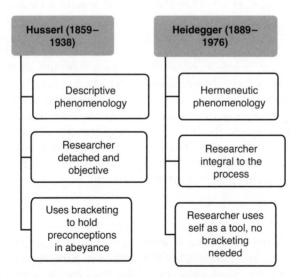

Figure 5.2 Descriptive and hermeneutic phenomenology.

exist in social settings. Grounded theory seeks to establish theory where none exists; for example, it is particularly useful in examining the experiences of new illnesses or the effects of new drugs. Glaser and Strauss used grounded theory to investigate the interactions of hospital staff with dying patients and it has been used more recently to investigate how people cope following a stroke (Kessler et al. 2009).

Grounded theory is perceived as truly inductive as data is generated 'from the ground' in the absence of theory. The researcher is perceived as a blank slate with no preconceived ideas to prove or disprove. Data emerges from the participants' stories so case histories or interviews are the preferred data collection methods. The key features of grounded theory are: the use of theoretical sampling and the constant comparative method of analysis. The researcher has no pre-constructed sampling frame but samples until the data related by the participants reaches a saturation point; that is, that no new data emerges. The researcher analyses the data concurrently by comparing and contrasting each participant's narrative with the previous ones and future ones. Although there is a concrete foundation that guides the structure of grounded theory, some conflict exists from the founders. This has resulted in conflicting directions and competing methodological approaches. For example, Glaser (1992) argues that there is no need to review any literature pertaining to the topic under study as it may contaminate the analysis. However, Strauss and Corbin (1990) disagree and argue that the literature adds another voice to the construction of ideas and uncovers some important contextual and political influences that can enhance understanding.

It is suggested in much of the literature that grounded theory is embedded in symbolic interactionism (Polit and Beck 2006), which claims that humans make life meaningful by cognitively using symbols such as language, social patterns, concepts, objects, etc. to construct culture and create interactions. This assumes that people respond to situations according to the meanings that they apply to them. These meanings depict what people perceive as acceptable and unacceptable practices. For health care, symbolic interactionism is useful if researchers want to understand the decision-making practices of various social groups so that the most appropriate care strategies can be applied. Mellion and Tovin (2002) used grounded theory to investigate physical therapy and Alsen et al. (2008) used this method to explore how patients perceived their illness post-myocardial-infarction.

Ethnography

Ethnography is derived from the Greek word *ethnos* meaning cultural group (LoBiondo-Wood and Haber 2010). It is rooted in anthropology and studies cultural patterns, life-ways and experiences. Ethnographers are interested in the extent to which people are influenced by the groups and culture in which they live. Ethnography is underpinned by a naturalist philosophy where the researcher enters the setting of those being studied through fieldwork. Ethnography contrasts with phenomenology regarding the research subject: phenomenology focuses on individual understandings whereas ethnography focuses on group understandings and interactions. There are some similarities with grounded theory in that symbols such as language, values and norms are acknowledged as relevant as the researcher strives to understand the cultural connotations associated with symbol. But grounded theory does not necessarily take place in the natural setting. In ethnographic research the researcher immerses themselves in the participant's world by closely interacting with them in their daily activities. Participant observation is the main method of data collection.

Ethnography has advantages in producing rich, deep, holistic data but is time-consuming and very labour intensive as infiltrating a culture requires trust and intimacy and these take time to develop. An example of this would be Whyte's (1955) study of an Italian slum in his book, *The Social Structure of an Italian Slum: Street Corner Society*. Whyte spent six years living with a family in Cornersville, an Italian slum, in order to observe the social structures and behaviour patterns. Although a level of intimacy develops, the researcher is still an 'outsider' to the group and the extent to which the interpretations of the researcher and the realities of participants 'match' is always open to debate. Another major drawback is the potential for a Hawthorne effect where participants change their behaviour because they are being observed. The term Hawthorne effect came from the Hawthorne plant of the Western Electric Corporation where a series of experiments regarding time and motion were conducted. The results showed that regardless of the change introduced productivity increased because the workers were being observed.

Ethnography is valuable to health care for a number of reasons:

- It enables healthcare professionals to understand why certain illnesses are more prevalent in some cultures than others and this in turn creates opportunities for health education.
- It can be used to rethink current policies and working practices; for example, Ballinger and Payne (2002) used ethnography over a five-week period to evaluate the ways in which risk was interpreted and managed in a day hospital for older people. The study found that risk management strategies disempowered older people as the regimes imposed upon them by healthcare professionals created an environment where they were dissuaded from performing independent activity that they would usually have performed at home. This has resulted in some hospitals reclassifying how risk is assessed.
- Ethnography is not only used to investigate other cultures but has been used to explore the culture of health care. For example, Griffiths

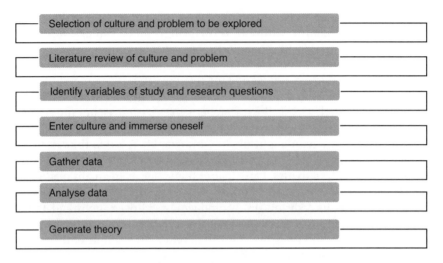

Selection of culture and problem to be explored

Literature review of culture and problem

Identify variables of study and research questions

Enter culture and immerse oneself

Gather data

Analyse data

Generate theory

Figure 5.3 Stages of ethnographic research.

(2008) used ethnography to explore the reality of the nurses role in an acute medical unit and Carr (1998) used it to study the protective role of families caring for hospitalized relatives. Studies such as these provide valuable insights of behaviour that can be transferred to understand other clinical situations and cultures.

Stages in ethnographic research

Garson (2008) describes the stages undertaken in ethnographic research (see Figure 5.3).

Exercise 5.3

Access the following three research articles and write some notes about your understanding of phenomenology, grounded theory and ethnography. Consider how the three methods are similar and how they differ.

Woodgate, R. (2000) An introduction to conducting qualitative research in children with cancer, *Journal of Paediatric Oncology Nursing*, 17(4): 207–28.

Ellett, M.C.C. and Beausang, C.C. (2002) Introduction to qualitative research, *Gastroenterology Nursing*, 25(1): 4–10.

Curtise, K.C. and White, P. (2005) Qualitative research design and approaches in radiography, *Radiography*, 11: 217–25.

Narratives

Narrative research is defined by Parker and Shotter (1990) as the verbal re-counting of life events through story telling. Cobley (2001) states that wherever you find humans, you will find stories. Some writers suggest that humans have a natural ability to tell stories; we grow up with stories from parents and teachers and we have to narrate experiences for many reasons throughout life. For example, every night on the world news people are telling their stories of tragic events or sharing emotional experiences, therefore it seems only natural that story telling should be an accepted method of gathering data from people. Subjective emotions are often neglected in quantitative research and yet they are a crucial part of human make-up and play a large role in how ill people communicate their needs in health care.

Narrative research draws on elements of interpretivist and constructivist philosophy in that story telling reflects reality from *that* speaker's point of view and is therefore constructed from *their* interpretation of *their* reality. Narratives are described as an empowering method of data collection as the position of the researcher is described as 'minimal' implying that they have a facilitative role rather than a directional one. In contrast to other research approaches that are researcher dominant, narrative approaches give the participants the power to direct the data. In this way the participants say what they want to say and not what the researcher wants to hear. Participants are free to express their feelings, they choose what is important rather than the researcher directing the process and selecting the questions.

There is evidence that story telling can be therapeutic; for example, counsellors have always used story telling as a means of encouraging clients to self problem solve by using discourse to uncover issues that need to be addressed. It is suggested that summarizing and organizing experiences helps clients/patients to understand better and move forward with therapy. Overcash (2004) found that story telling increased cancer sufferers sense of self-worth and personal validation as patients felt that they had been listened to. Holloway and Freshwater (2007) claim that the narrative researcher occupies a privileged location in the therapeutic process and claim that story telling can be a useful coping strategy as story telling allows the intentions and motivations to be uncovered and analysed.

Frank (1995) identifies three types of narrative that are relevant to health care:

- restitution narrative where participants discuss how they got well from their illness or are able to be empowered during illness such as in an expert patient programme;
- chaos narrative where participants are chronically ill and discuss their suffering such as in a chronic pain support group;

- quest narrative where people have suffered an experience and learned from it and now wish to educate others about what they have learned; for example, a person with an alcohol problem in an AA meeting may use this approach to help others in the group.

The main criticisms of narrative research are that it is anecdotal and not generalizable to other people or situations; however, qualitative researchers view this as a strength rather than a weakness as validity is more relevant than reliability. Parahoo (2006) highlights that if a study is performed well it can have value beyond the sample studied as there are usually some elements of narrative that other people can identify with. For health care even narratives that are analysed individually have relevance as patients should be assessed and cared for according to their individual needs and this involves attending to their individual stories. However, stories are not necessarily factual constructions as variables such as illness, cognition and memory can impact the authenticity.

Case studies

Case studies are often positioned in the qualitative sections of research books but contain elements of both qualitative and quantitative research. Although multiple methods can be employed such as interviews, diaries and observations, a case study is usually defined as a retrospective investigation into a written case or event. Either one or several cases can be examined at any one time as part of the case study. A single case does not necessarily relate to one person but may refer to a family, a social group or an organization. The quantity of cases that are examined is usually small due to the intensity of the investigation that is required; however, the strength of this method lies in the depth of analysis that is possible. As with narratives, the reliance on memory when reconstructing a case history can result in data being distorted or selectively retrieved. This results in crucial data being excluded from the study.

Case studies may be regarded as interpretivist and constructivist as they involve analysing descriptions and constructing theory but they also have an objective element as the researcher is often removed from the participant. This can have advantages for health care as case studies permit investigation into otherwise inaccessible situations that could be deemed unethical by other methods of study and allow researchers to explore sensitive topics where other forms of investigation could produce emotional pain, embarrassment or trauma. For example, when Irving (2002) used case studies to examine the unethical use of restraints, she used the hospital as her 'case' and James et al. (2007) used the case study method to explore how a family copes when a family member dies from cancer. Case studies have also been used to examine the working patterns of organizations such as the longitudinal study carried out by Korman and Glennester (1990) who investigated the events that led to the closure of Darenth Park Hospital in 1988. They may also be useful for generating hypotheses or disease patterns that can be investigated quantitatively.

Stake (2000) identified three types of case studies: intrinsic, instrumental and collective.

- In **intrinsic** case studies the researcher just seeks to gain a deeper understanding of the particular case in order to tease out the lived experience. For example, Doucherty et al. (2006) used this method to explore symptom distress in children being treated for cancer.
- In **instrumental** case studies the researcher focuses on a particular issue or generalization in order to give a deep and focused analysis. An example of this type of case study would be Freud's ([1909] 2001) case study into 'Little Hans'. Little Hans was a 5-year-old boy who developed a severe phobia of horses. Freud diagnosed that this phobia was a symptom of the Oedipus complex, implying that Little Hans wished to stay inside near his mother rather than be exposed to external influences.
- In a **collective** case study the instrumental study is extended to include several cases that pertain to the phenomena being studied. Comparing and contrasting case studies allows relationships, processes and social patterns to be identified. Furthermore, unlike quantitative surveys and experiments that only provide a stilled snapshot of processes, the nature of the processes can be studied over a longer period of time which may uncover deeper meaning and more holistic data.

The type and number of cases included in a study is dependent upon the purpose of the enquiry. Large case studies have their advantages in replicability and reliability but Stake points out that using more than one case may dilute the importance and meaning of the experience.

Action research

Action research was developed by Kurt Lewin in 1946 and as the title suggests it is a combination of research and action. The purpose of action research is to improve the quality of care by implementing sustainable change. Bowling (2009) describes action research as a method of generating knowledge about a social system while simultaneously trying to change it. She describes two key features: improvement and involvement. In some ways action research is ethnographic as it involves the researcher being in the field and forging

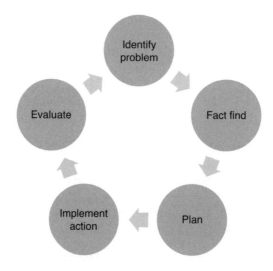

Figure 5.4 The action research cycle.

close relationships with the participants. However, the researcher's role is facilitative rather than directional in that they encourage and guide staff to look for their own solutions.

Stringer (1996) describes three very simple stages to action research: look, think, act. However, most researchers describe it as a cyclical process that involves five stages (see Figure 5.4). Discussion of each of the five stages follows:

1   *Identifying a research problem* The need for an action research project is practice driven as the problem often arises from the realization that practice needs improvement and that the practice is amenable to change. At this stage the researcher may be brought in as an observer in order to evaluate the extent of the problem, the real nature of the problem and the genuine need for change. The researcher identifies issues or problems from the observations and shares these with the participants.

2   *Fact finding* This involves the providers of care reflecting upon: what they do, how they do it and why they do it in a particular way. The participants and the researcher then access research based evidence to investigate the problem and the potential solutions. Questionnaires, interviews or focus groups can be used to gather data that is then fed back to the group for validation purposes prior to planning any change. This gives staff the chance to discuss the findings, refine their own perceptions and clarify the researcher's interpretations.

The focus is on helping healthcare professionals to critically explore the situation they are in and develop their own understanding of the organization. Bowling refers to this process as rapid appraisal as it involves speedily gaining insight into the research community.

3   *Plan the proposed change* Once the areas for investigation are understood and the solutions have been critically debated a plan of change is proposed. The researcher facilitates meetings that involve:
  • setting goals;
  • ascertaining roles and responsibilities;
  • agreeing priorities and time frames;
  • identifying barriers;
  • accessing resources.

4   *Implement the change* This involves the whole team using an evidence based approach to implement new methods of delivery. The collaborative nature of this process is described by Bowling (2009) as empowering to all of the members involved as the researcher and the participants democratically enter into dialogue where they exchange their knowledge and expertise. This shared approach encourages a feeling of ownership and emancipation. However, Parahoo (2006) points out that in reality the degree of participation varies according to the knowledge and skills of those involved.

5   *Evaluate the change* This stage involves collecting data to establish the impact of the change. This can be done qualitatively through interviews or focus groups or quantitatively through the use of a survey.

Action research has gained popularity in the healthcare arena in recent years due to the potential for rapid change and real world applicability. Conventional research often takes several months or years before it finds its way into practice but action research has an immediate impact as it takes place in the here and now. For example, Bridges and Meyer (2007) used action research to study the introduction of inter-professional care coordinators (IPCCs) in an inner-city London hospital and found that the IPCCs were taking on care nursing work without adequate training. Action research helped to identify training needs and reorganized tasks. This approach can also help to bridge the theory–practice gap as practitioners are encouraged to integrate research into their everyday activity; in this way, evidence based practice becomes the norm. Action research has a number of limitations including getting all of those involved in the project to perceive problems and solutions in the same way. The greater the number of people that are involved in a project, the greater the potential for conflict. Ethical issues are also possible as in conventional research participants have a choice in whether to participate but as action research is collaborative, some participants may feel coerced into participating.

Sampling for qualitative research

Unlike quantitative research that seeks to generalize findings to the wider population, qualitative research is about accepting the existence of multiple realities so generalizability is not a concern. For this reason sample sizes tend to be much smaller than those used in quantitative studies. Qualitative studies use non-probability sampling which means that participants are selected by non-randomized methods. In qualitative research selective sampling is a practical necessity as participants are selected according to their potential to provide rich, meaningful data. Three types of non-probability sampling are used: purposive sampling, convenience sampling and snowballing, which we will now go on to explore.

Purposive sampling

Purposive sampling involves consciously selecting participants according to their knowledge base. As the name suggests, researchers purposely handpick the participants according to predefined criteria. This type of sampling is also referred to as *judgmental* sampling as the researcher makes decisions regarding the appropriateness of the sample. The researcher selects inclusion and exclusion criteria to determine which participants will yield the most knowledge. For example, Kealey and Mcintyre (2005) used purposive sampling to study occupational therapy services. They identified inclusion criteria which included: only adults aged 18 years or over who understand written and spoken English, those who have an informal carer, those in the palliative stage of illness and those who had been referred for domiciliary occupational health services in the community. Purposive sampling can be used to study unusual groups such as those with rare diseases or particular ethnic groups. Phenomenologists and narrative researchers usually select to use this sampling method as the chosen participants are 'purposeful' to the topic being investigated. Grounded theory uses a type of purposive sampling called theoretical sampling which basically means that the theory guides the sample selection. Theoretical sampling usually involves using 20–40 people who are best able to contribute to the evolving theory. Sampling, data collection and analysis occur concurrently and sampling continues until no new data is generated and saturation is achieved.

Convenience sampling

It is not always possible for a researcher to gain access to a sampling frame, for example if few people have the relevant knowledge or accessibility is problematic, or time is a crucial factor. In these cases the researcher may have to select the most readily available people who meet the inclusion and exclusion criteria. This means selecting participants who are accessible and convenient. This approach is often referred to as accidental or volunteer sampling as it is a favourite method used by market researchers. In health care it could be used to sample every patient who attended a specific clinic on a particular day or every patient who receives a particular intervention. For example, Swartz (2010) investigated the effectiveness of a tight-fitting mask in the delivery of nebulised treatment and used a convenience sample of eight paediatric patients admitted to her clinic. Despite the small sample, this study led to a change in the way that therapy was administered to children in both hospital and community settings. This is the least reliable form of sampling and the participants are rarely representative of the wider population; however, it is useful when access to populations is limited.

Snowball sampling

Snowball sampling is often referred to as *network* sampling as social networks are used to recruit participants. The researcher selects a few participants and asks these participants to locate further participants for the study who then also nominate people and a network of participants develops or a snowballing effect occurs. A weakness of this approach is that the sample could be restricted to a small network. Another drawback is the potential for bias as participants select members who are known to them.

Exercise 5.4

Read the following article:

> Innes, J.M. (1998) A qualitative insight into the experiences of post-graduate radiography students: causes of stress and methods of coping, *Radiography*, 4(2), 89–100.

Answer the following questions:

1 What were the inclusion and exclusion criteria in the study?
2 What form of sampling was used?
3 Was the sampling size appropriate for the study?

This section has briefly introduced the three types of sampling that are used in qualitative studies. A limitation of each type of non-probability sampling is the potential for bias and the inability to generalize the findings due to small sample sizes. Whichever strategy is selected, the researcher should adequately describe and justify the sampling strategy that has been used. This should include:

- the type of sampling;
- the inclusion and exclusion criteria;
- the sample size and sampling frame;
- the demographic characteristics of the sample.

Data collection methods

Qualitative research explores feelings, perceptions and attitudes, therefore data collection methods need to demonstrate their ability to meet these objectives. Achieving the depth and richness of data that is necessary requires the researcher to engage with participants on a social level. The three types of data collection methods that tend to be used are interviews, focus groups and observations.

Interviews

Interviews involve asking questions and recording the respondents' answers. They can be carried out face to face, via the telephone, via Skype on the internet or via a video conference. Telephone interviews and face-to-face interviews have a long and established history; for example, Parahoo (2006) states that telephone interviewing is the most dominant form of interviewing in the United States. However, telephone respondents tend to be less cooperative than those who are interviewed face to face and the suitability of the internet has yet to be established. Interviews can be described as structured, semi-structured or unstructured according to the depth of data that is required. In structured interviews the content is standardized and rigidly controlled by the researcher. The interviewer has an interview schedule that guides the order and content of the questions. An example of a structured interview would be where a nurse assesses a patient using a structured assessment tool such as Unified Assessment or Roper, Logan and Tierney's model. The aim is to strive for uniformity and consistency; if every nurse used a different assessment tool, the result would be confusion and meaningless assessment data. Questions usually progress from broad to specific topics and usually start with the safe issues before progressing to more sensitive ones. This method is considered the most reliable method of interviewing but the depth of response is often limited.

Semi-structured interviews are considered the most democratic method of interviewing as both the researcher and the participants have some control over the content. In semi-structured interviews the participants are asked a series of broad questions that encourage them to express their feelings, perceptions and experiences. In order to keep the interviews flowing, the researcher can use a topic guide that keeps the conversation focused on the topic area. The topic guide is not as rigid as the interview guide that would be used in a structured interview and the aim is to enhance flexibility rather than uniformity.

In unstructured interviews the participants totally direct the content of the interview and the researcher is the receiver of data. It could be argued that there is no such thing as an unstructured interview as the researcher always has an element of control and has already selected the research question that will dictate the agenda. The role of the researcher in this type of interviewing is to keep the conversation flowing by probing and clarifying the responses. This type of interview has been criticized as stressful for participants as they may dry up or become tired, and stressful for the researcher as it is difficult to be passive when they own the research agenda. However, there is less potential for interviewer bias as the researcher has little opportunity to reveal their own values.

As most healthcare professionals use interviews as part of the assessment process, the techniques of interviewing should be familiar and the healthcare researcher should be sufficiently skilled. However, Burns and Grove (2005) point out that using this technique for research is far more sophisticated and requires sensitive communication skills as the interviewer can never predict the participant's response to a question. A question perceived as safe to the interviewer may be damaging to the participant. The interviewer needs to prepare strategies for dealing with potential distress prior to the study.

Reflective activity

Reflect upon the communication skills that you use to assess patients/clients.

What skills do you think that the researcher would require when carrying out interviews?

How are the communication skills different?

Consider that the aim of assessment in health care is to establish a therapeutic relationship but in research the aim is to acquire data quickly and effectively.

Bowling (2009) describes interviews as the least burdensome method of data collection as they only require the respondents to speak the same language as the researcher and understand the questions that are asked. Participants with limited literacy skills can be included. In some cases it may be necessary to video the interview in order to preserve contextual elements and interpret the participant's body language; however, Ellis (2010) points out that this technique may increase the vulnerability of the participants and increase their stress levels. Powney and Watts (1987) highlight the irony of performing interviews by stating that the strength of interviews lies in the 'talking' but the very process of being interviewed impacts the dynamic quality of the narrative. They claim that the 'talk' belongs to the participant's unique experience and cannot be translated in a truly meaningful way. Methodological rigour can be enhanced through the additional use of reflexive journals and field notes although conflict exists regarding when these should be written. Crookes and Davies (2004) point out that writing field notes at the time of the interview distances the researcher from the participant; however, waiting until after the interview results in data being forgotten.

The strength of interviews is in the depth of data that can be produced; however, the sample needs to be reasonably small or analysis becomes too cumbersome. As rich data is required, interviews are often very time consuming. For ethical security, ground rules concerning confidentiality and anonymity need to be established and institutional lone worker policies need to be adhered to.

Focus groups

> Group conversations are a common feature of human interaction. Through them we find that some people share our views and experiences and others do not. It is an important way to socialise, share ideas and learn about how other people think and feel. It is no wonder then that some researchers believe that bringing a group of people together to discuss particular questions can be a useful way of generating knowledge.
>
> (Parahoo 2006: 5)

Interviews have been acknowledged as time consuming, and a different strategy identified for qualitative research projects that produces data more rapidly is focus groups. Focus groups allow the researcher to access the collective views of groups of people and are described by Redmond and Curtis (2009) as a form of group interview that is humanistic and exploratory. The aim of a focus group is to create an environment that encourages participants to express a range of different perspectives about a particular topic. Researchers are not just interested in what is said by the participants but in how they say it, the language that is used and the intensity of the feelings that are expressed. Focus groups usually require a facilitator to maintain the focus of the topic and keep conversation flowing and a co-facilitator who observes behaviour patterns, body language and context. As with individual interviews, the researcher acts as an instrument and uses an interview guide. The guide needs to be sufficiently flexible in order to encourage freedom to speak but specific enough to maintain the focus of the topic as increasing the number of participants can lead to diversions.

The characteristics of the focus group participants are usually decided by the purpose of the study; inclusion and exclusion criteria are strictly adhered to and the sample is chosen purposively so that the group are knowledgeable and homogenous in terms of their background and experiences. Selecting a homogenous sample ensures that each member of the group is able to participate but allows for individuality. However, there are no set rules and Redmond and Curtis (2009) highlight that sometimes using heterogeneous samples that differ can also be advantageous and can produce more interesting results. Sometimes it makes sense to group people together who can offer diverse views.

Another factor that should be considered when examining focus groups is whether the group should consist of acquaintances or strangers. Existing groups can be more comfortable and enhance the participants' confidence to express their views but may contain power structures that could inhibit their willingness to communicate. Established groups may also have behavioural norms that could impact the spontaneity and disclosure of data. Howatson-Jones (2007) used an existing group of nurses in her focus group when she explored the learning behaviours of qualified nurses. She separated the nurses into groups according to whether they were studying at diploma or degree level. Problems were encountered regarding response rates and willingness to participate as over-emphasizing ethical rights resulted in only seven participants responding. Under-representation by males, different educational preparation in overseas nurses and the low response rate led to the groups becoming pilots for a larger study.

Some variation exists in the literature regarding the optimum size for a focus group. Some authors suggest six to ten (Bloor et al. 2001) while others have used as few as three (Pugsley 1996). Ellis (2010) states that an effective focus group should consist of between six to twelve participants as managing any more than this becomes too challenging, particularly if there are dominant members or sensitive topic areas. Ellis recommends that a focus group should last for approximately two hours. This said, Kruger and Casey (2000) warn that focus groups can be physiologically and psychologically tiring and advise that two hours should be the limit.

Focus groups also pose ethical dilemmas as there is no opportunity for anonymity or confidentiality. However, these can be enhanced through the use of internet focus groups which take place in virtual environments such as *illuminate* where participants interact through the use of an online discussion room. This method has advantages in cost reduction and accessing participants but may exclude the less technologically able people that may have valuable data to give. They are also hard to moderate as the researcher is not physically present and if the data becomes sensitive or uncomfortable it is harder for the researcher to intervene.

Exercise 5.5

From the discussion so far, compose a list of the advantages and disadvantages of focus groups. Some suggestions are provided in the Appendix.

Observations

Observations are considered crucial to naturalistic research and can be classified as *non-participant observations* where the observer is outside of the research context and *participant observation* where the researcher infiltrates the participant's daily life and becomes part of the environment.

Non-participant observation

In non-participant observation or 'complete' observation the researcher occupies a passive role that centres on gathering data in an objective way either overtly (openly) or covertly (unseen). Obtaining data by covert means enables the researcher to view reality that is free from distortion or Hawthorne effects but can be perceived as spying or policing by the participants. This approach can also lead to feelings of discomfort in both the researcher and the group; for example, Jun (2008) used a covert approach to study the gambling practices of women in Ontario. By assuming a covert research role he was able to observe the natural behaviour of female gamblers without fear of them changing their habits due to his presence. He was able to ascertain how much money women spend on gambling, how they feel about their habit and how their gambling impacts their family dynamics. Jun's ethical principles led to feelings of anxiety when women began to feel sorry for him which resulted in his decision to make his role overt. Unfortunately this resulted in the participants refusing to communicate openly. Jun (2008: 100) stated:

> Regardless of my efforts, the overt approach I attempted was unsuccessful because my research disclosure immediately changed social relationships and silenced voices. They started to view me differently, treating me as a suspicious outsider who should not be trusted because I did not share their experiences.

In non-participant observation the researcher occupies the role of an outsider and maintains a critical distance from the group. This critical distance gives the researcher the opportunity to record observations as and when they occur so that data is fresh and less affected by memory disturbances. Jun found that critical distance gave him the psychological space needed for authentic observations.

Observational techniques have been criticized for their covert and unethical approaches as the researcher sets out to deliberately deceive the participants. Secondly, many of the participants have not consented to be part of the research and modern ethics committees are now uncomfortable approving such studies. Most researchers advocate an open approach arguing that it is morally and practically better this way. Haralambos and Holborne (2000) state that the open researcher may be able to avoid participation in distasteful, immoral or illegal behaviour. For example, when studying Liverpool delinquents in his book *View from the Boys* Howard Parker (1974) refused to participate in the theft of car radios without harming his relationship with the group that he was studying. The main disadvantage of being open is the potential for a Hawthorne effect as those being observed change their behaviour.

Participant observation

In participant observation the researcher participates in the activities of the group being observed, hence the researcher observes from within the group. The insider perspective is also known as the *emic* perspective and is particularly useful when the researcher seeks to understand cultural beliefs and social groups. Goffman's (1961) study into mental health institutions is a classic study that used participant observations. Goffman obtained employment as a member of staff in order to investigate institutional practices. In participant observation studies the researcher initially seeks out the most knowledgeable informants and uses snowballing as a means of gaining further insights. Participant observation has advantages over interviews as the researcher can experience reality rather than relying on reports that can be distorted or forgotten. Of course one could ask the question, why is the researcher's report of reality any more valid than anyone else's?

Techniques such as audio recording, video recording, podcasting and taking field notes are usually used because the primary aim is to retain as much of the context as possible. The role of the researcher is that of passive observer rather than an active expert. This role is crucial to the 'fitting in' and gaining trust processes. Learning the group's language and acting in similar ways are identified by Ellis (2010) as key features; however, Whyte (1955) found that imitating the group's behaviour could be detrimental to trust and instead found that behaving naturally generated more trust and greater cooperation.

Over-involvement or 'going native' has been identified as one of the hazards of participant observation as this can negatively impact the objectivity required for the role. Savage (2000) experienced problems with going native in her study of nurses' therapeutic relationships with patients. She took part in nursing activities that were within her sphere of competence in order to be useful and found that she changed her body language and began to use touch in ways that she had previously perceived as inappropriate.

A further weakness of participant observation is the risk to the researcher, especially if they are observing covertly. For example, one researcher studying Glasgow gangs was unable to reveal his true identity as he feared for his personal safety. One of the main limitations of observations concerns the extent to which it can be replicated as real life cannot be relived again for the sake of research. Despite the criticisms, observations provide valuable insights into phenomena that are usually hidden from public view such as in Paradis's (2000) study into homeless women, Quirk and Lelliott's (2002) ethnographic study into life on acute psychiatric wards and Allan's (2006) research into nurses' emotions while working in a fertility clinic.

Summary

This chapter has identified the key features of and studies used to undertake qualitative research. The philosophical underpinnings, sampling methods and data collection techniques have been discussed. Three major philosophical viewpoints have been identified and each one has been linked to a specific type of research and data collection process. For example, the naturalist approach has been linked to ethnography and observations in order to demonstrate how and why qualitative researchers explore people in their natural settings. It has been argued that patients do not exist in institutions and most of their illness takes place within their cultural setting, therefore studying behaviours in these settings has great relevance for health care. People interpret symptoms and illness behaviour in many different ways so phenomenology has a role in enabling researchers to understand the interpretations that people place on behaviours and feelings. Healthcare professionals assess patients through the stories that they narrate and the relevance of narratives has been established. Action research has been described as an empowering approach to research that facilitates growth for researchers, patients and the institution. The rationality for small, selective sampling techniques has been discussed. We can conclude that vast amounts of data are collected and this requires careful analysis in order to preserve the context and meaning of the information. The next chapter will explore how this data can be analysed in ways that preserve the meaning and enhance the rigour of the work.

Reflective activity

Consider the advantages and disadvantages of interviews, focus groups and observations for healthcare research.

Which data collection method appears to be most suited for your particular clinical area? Consider why this is the case. This exercise will enhance your critical thinking skills when appraising literature that uses these techniques.

Jargon busting

Make a list of any words in this chapter that you do not understand. Look up their meaning and consider their use in the world of research. You may identify some of the following words and terms:

Anecdotal: Informal and unvalidated evidence told from one person to another.

Authentic: Real.

Bracketing: Acknowledging personal beliefs and knowledge and feelings about the topic area and putting them aside until after data has been analysed so that the researcher's views do not bias the study.

Constructivism: A way of thinking that assumes that people build up their understanding of the world in small sections based upon their experiences.

Emic: Studying groups as an insider, becoming part of the group.

Ethnography: The study of people in their natural settings.

Etic: Studying people as an outsider to the group.

Facilitative: The researcher adopts a helping and guiding role.

Hawthorne effect: This is where people change their behaviour due to being part of a study.

Heterogeneous: The sample have a wide variety of characteristics that make them different from each other.

Heurmeneutic: A form of phenomenology devised by Heidegger that is cyclical and believes that the researcher is an integral part of the study and uses their skills as an instrument.

Homogenous: The extent to which a sample have the same characteristics so that the sample appear to be very similar to each other.

Interpretivism: A way of thinking that has its roots in the ways in which people perceive and undestand events and behaviours.

Naturalism: A way of thinking that assumes that people can only be understood in their natural setting so that culture and context can be captured as part of the data.

Non-probability sampling: The selection of a sample that uses non-random methods.

Phenomena: Things that occur or exist in the world.

Phenomenology: A qualitative approach to research that explores people's experiences.

Philosophical: Thinking about the nature of the world, how and why things exist in the way that they do.

Purposive sampling: The researcher selects a sample purposefully and consciously.

Symbolic interactionism: This is a way of thinking that assumes that people use symbols as ways of associating meaning. Examples of symbols could be language, clothing, jewellery, tattoos.

References

Allan, H.T. (2006) Using participant observation to immerse oneself in the field, *Journal of Research in Nursing*, 11(5): 397–407.

Alsen, P. Brink, E. and Persson, L.O. (2008) Patients illness perceptions four months after a myocardial infarction, *Journal of Clinical Nursing*, 17(5): 25–33.

Ballinger, C. and Payne, S. (2002) The construction of the risk of falling among and by older people, *Ageing and Society*, 22: 305–42.

Bloor, M., Frankland, J. and Thomas, M. (2001) *Focus Groups in Social Research.* Sage: London.

Bowling, A. (2009) *Research Methods in Healthcare: Investigating Health and Health Services*. Maidenhead: Open University Press.

Bridges, J. and Meyer, J. (2007) New workforce roles in healthcare, *Journal of Health Organization and Management*, 21(4): 381–92.

Burns, N. and Grove, S. (2005) *The Practice of Nursing Research: Conduct, Critique and Utilization*. St Louis, M.: Elsevier Saunders.

Carr, J.M. (1998) Vigilance as caring, *Nursing Science Quarterly*, 11(12): 74–8.

Cobley, P. (2001) *Narratives: An Introduction*. London: Routledge.

Coombs, C.R., Park, J.R., Loan-Clarke, J. et al. (2003) Perceptions of radiography and the NHS: a qualitative study, *Radiography*, 9(2): 109–22.

Crookes, P.A. and Davies, S. (2004) *Research into Practice: Essential Skills for Reading and Applying Research in Nursing and Healthcare*. London: Bailliere Tindall.

Doucherty, N.M., Strauss, M.E., Duizeo, T. and St Hilaire, A. (2006) The cognitive origins of specific types of schizophrenic speech disorders, *American Journal of Psychiatry*, 163: 2111–18.

Ellis, P. (2010) *Understanding Research for Nursing Students*. Exeter: Learning Matters Ltd.

Frank, A.W. (1995) *The Wounded Story Teller: Body, Illness and Ethics*. Chicago: University of Chicago Press.

Freud, S. ([1909, 2001]) *The Standard Edition of the Complete Works of Sigmund Frend*. London: Vantage.

Gadamer, H.G. (1976) *Philosophical Hermeneutics*. Berkeley, CA: University of California Press.

Garson, D. (2008) The ethnographic paradigm, *Administration Science Quarterly*, 24: 527–38.

Glaser, B.G. and Strauss, A. (1967) *The Discovery of Grounded Theory: Strategies for Qualitative Research*. New York: Hawthorne.

Glaser, B.G. (1992) Emergence vs Forcing: Basics of Grounded Theory Analysis. Mill Valley: Sociology Press.

Goffman, E. (1961) *Asylums: Essays on the Social Situation of Mental Patients and Other Inmates*. London: Penguin.

Griffiths, P. (2008) Nursing patients in transition. Understanding the context of practice. Paper presented at the Royal College of Nursing. Conference, Royal College of Nursing, London.

Haralambos, M. and Holborne, M. (2000) *Sociology: Themes and Perspectives*. London: Collins Educational.

Heidegger, M. (1962) *Time and Being*. New York: Harperone.

Holloway, I. and Freshwater, D. (2007) Vulnerable story telling: narrative research in nursing, *Journal of Research in Nursing*, 12(6): 703–11.

Howatson-Jones, I.L. (2007) Dilemmas of focus group recruitment and implementation: a pilot perspective, *Nurse Researcher*, 14(2): 7–17.

Innes, J.M. (1998) A qualitative insight into the experiences of post graduate radiography students: causes of stress and methods of coping, *Radiography*, 4(2): 89–100.

Irving, K. (2002) Governing the conduct of conduct: are restraints inevitable? *Journal of Advanced Nursing*, 40(4): 405–12.

James, I., Andershed, B. and Ternestedt, B. (2007) A family's beliefs about cancer, dying and death in the end of life, *Journal of Family Nursing*, 13: 226–53.

Jun, L. (2008) Ethical challenges in participant observation: a reflection on ethnographic fieldwork, *The Qualitative Report*, 13(1): 100–15.

Kealey, P. and McIntyre, I. (2005) An evaluation of the domiciliary occupational therapy service in palliative cancer care in a community trust, *European Journal of Cancer Care*, 14(3): 232–43.

Kessler, D., Dubouloz, C.J., Urbanowski, R. and Egan, M. (2009) Meaning perspective transformation following stroke: the process of change, *Disability and Rehabilitation*, 31(13): 1056–65.

Korman, N. and Glennester, H. (1990) *Hospital Closure: A Political and Economic Study*. Buckingham: Open University Press.

Kruger, R.A. and Casey, M.A. (2000) *Focus Groups: A Practical Guide for Applied Research*. London: Sage.

Laverty, M. (2003) Hermeneutic phenomenology and phenomenology: a comparison of historical and methodological considerations, *International Journal of Qualitative Methods*, 2(3): 21–35.

LoBiondo-Wood, G. and Haber, J. (2010) *Nursing Research*. St Louis, MI: Mosby.

Mellion, L.R. and Tovin, M.M. (2002) Grounded theory, a qualitative research methodology for physical therapy, *Physiotherapy and Practice*, 18(3): 109–20.

Overcash, J.A. (2004) Narrative research. A viable methodology for clinical nursing, *Nursing Forum*, 39(1): 15–22.

Paradis, E.K. (2000) Feminist and community psychology ethics in research with homeless women, *American Journal of Community Psychology*, 28: 839–58.

Parahoo, K. (2006) *Nursing Research: Principles, Process and Issues*. Basingstoke: Palgrave macmillan.

Parker, H.J. (1974) *View from the Boys: Sociology of Downtown Adolescents.* Newton Abbott: David and Charles.

Parker, I. and Shotter, J. (1990) *Deconstructing Social Psychology.* London: Routledge.

Polit, D.F. and Beck, C. (2006) *Essentials of Nursing Research: Appraising Evidence for Nursing Practice.* Philadelphia, PA: Lippincott, Williams and Wilkins.

Powney, J. and Watts, M. (1987) *Interviewing in Educational Research.* London: Routledge.

Pugsley, L. (1996) *Focus, groups, young people and sex education,* in: R. Redmond and E. Curtis (2009) Focus groups: Principles and process, *Nurse Researcher,* 16(3), 57–69.

Quirk, A. and Lelliott, P. (2002) A participant observation study of life on an acute psychiatric ward, *The Psychiatrist,* 26: 344–8.

Redmond, R. and Curtis, E. (2009) Focus groups: principles and process, *Nurse Researcher,* 16(3): 57–69.

Savage, J. (2000) Ethnography and healthcare, *British Medical Journal,* 321: 1400–2.

Stake, R.E. (2000) *Case Studies,* in: N.K. Denzin and Y.S. Lincoln (2005) *Handbook of Qualitative Research.* California: Sage.

Strauss, A. and Corbin, J. (1990) *Basics of Qualitative Research: Grounded Theory Procedures and Techniques.* London: Sage.

Stringer, E.T. (1996) *Action Research: A Handbook for Practitioners.* London: Sage.

Swartz, C. (2010) *Blow-by versus face mask for infant paediatric nebulisation treatments,* in: M.M. Kirkpatrick McLaughlin and S.A. Bulla. *Real Stories of Nursing Research.* London: Jones and Bartlett.

Whyte, W. (1955) *The Social Structure of an Italian Slum: Street Corner Society.* Chicago: Chicago University Press.

6   Qualitative analysis

Introduction

Analysis of qualitative data is an inductive process as theory is generated after the process of data collection. Parahoo (2006) describes qualitative analysis as a lonely journey as the volume of data that is produced results in this stage of the research process being the most time-consuming and the most cognitively exhausting. Unlike quantitative data analysis which focuses on numbers, qualitative analysis examines words, descriptions and social processes. The analysis follows an interpretive process that allows words, motives, sequences and processes to be validated as ultimately truthful. This chapter will discuss the stages of analysis and the most common methods of qualitative data analysis, which are:

- content analysis
- thematic analysis
- the constant comparative method.

Some common models used for analysis will also be included and their relevance to health care will be examined.

Learning outcomes

At the end of this chapter you will be able to:

- identify the major methods that are used to analyse qualitative research;
- describe the key features of each approach to data analysis;

- link each approach to the most appropriate research methodology;
- describe the advantages and disadvantages of computer assisted software.

The stages of analysis

Although qualitative research has been described as less scientific than quantitative research it should not be any less rigorous or systematic; this implies that a set procedure must be applied in the same way to all of the data being analysed. The analysis must be empirically based or it may not be classified as research. As the data is not collected in numerical form it does not require statistical analysis but it requires analysis all the same. The style of analysis used will vary according to the research design but some techniques are common to all approaches; for example, all approaches require the researcher to:

- transcribe each recorded narrative verbatim (exactly as it is expressed by the participant, word for word);
- immerse themselves in the data by reading and re-reading the transcripts and subjectively interpret the text;
- make the data more manageable by breaking it down into parts and use a method of coding to compare and contrast the data;
- group data together to form themes or categories;
- put the data together to create theory.

Each of these stages will be discussed in more depth in this chapter, starting below.

1 Transcribing the data

The researcher collects data in a raw form through digitally recorded conversations, video or via internet facilities such as Skype. These narratives are virtually impossible to analyse in their verbal form so transcribing the conversations provides a written record that can be segmented and rebuilt visually. Transcription is very labour intensive as each narrative should be transcribed verbatim; this means that every word should be recorded exactly as it is spoken as soon after the data collection as possible to prevent loss of context. All pauses, expressions and exclamations need to be included. Bowling (2009) states that using symbols to indicate certain behaviours can be useful. For example, some researchers underscore the text to highlight when a participant raises their voice or stresses a certain word; others use bracket signs to highlight when multiple speakers are talking over each other.

Exercise 6.1

Ask a colleague the following question: 'How do you think that people can make themselves unhealthy?'. Write down their answer verbatim using the following code:

```
- = pause, {} = said in a fast way, [] = said slower,
  ! = raised voice, ** = added emphasis
~ = looked away from the questioner, & performed
  a hand gesture, < > = describe any
  body language.
```

Reflect upon how easy or difficult this process was and identify any problems.

The issue regarding who should transcribe the text is often debated by researchers. As transcribing is a labour-intensive process some researchers advocate that a research assistant should perform this task. The inclusion of an external transcriber should be included in the ethical approval and confidentiality needs to be maintained. Some researchers argue that using a transcriber detaches the researcher from the data and fragments the interpretation process; they advocate that the researcher should immerse themselves in the data in order to produce a study that can be termed holistic. The data from some digital recorders can be uploaded onto a computer and automatically transcribed. This reduces time and does not require an additional researcher but may also be criticized as removing the researcher from the data. Software such as *HyperTRANSCRIBE* enables words to be converted into text from digital recorders or MP3 players.

2 Immersion in the data

Once the data has been transcribed the researcher immerses themselves in the data by reading and re-reading the text in order to open up the data. During this stage the researcher writes descriptive statements about the raw data in an attempt to identify similarities and differences. For example, statements may be made about the intensity of certain comments or words or about the consistency of the statements made. The context in which comments were made may be highlighted in order to demonstrate the relevance of specific text so that comparisons can be made.

Exercise 6.2

Refer back to the text that you have identified from your colleague and identify any statements that are similar or different from each other.

---

3 Making the data manageable by coding

This stage of the analysis builds on the descriptive phase by breaking the sentences down into meaning units: this involves fragmenting the data into as many small parts as possible. This can be done by breaking the data down line by line and identifying relevant words or phrases which are then placed into groups. Straus and Corbin (1998) identified three stages to coding:

- open coding – where the major concepts and key words are identified;
- axial coding – which identifies patterns from the data. The data is then organized into categories and sub-categories;
- selective coding – where data is integrated to produce theory.

For example, open codes are very simple and often involve one word or very short phrases. An example could be:

'I came into physiotherapy because I wanted to help people to mobilize quickly but find that most of my job seems to be banging on people's chests'.

Open codes could be identified as:

- helping
- mobilizing
- banging on chests

Exercise 6.3

Can you identify any codes from the text that you have been analysing from the conversation with your colleague?

In axial coding the data is grouped together to form a category termed 'roles of the physiotherapist' and this data could form part of the axial coding process. One of the key issues when considering the coding process concerns the issue of validity and the extent to which the researcher's interpretation of the data matches the participant' meaning. Parahoo (2006) refers to this as face validity or content validity as it relates to the degree to which the items adequately reflect the phenomena under investigation. Different researchers use different methods of assurance; for example, Forhan et al. (2010) and Orpen and Harris (2010) both used the processes of member checking. This is where the codes are referred back to the participants for evaluation. Parahoo (2006) refers to this process as respondent validation. Moule et al. (2008) used multiple researchers who each analysed and coded the data privately. Comparisons were made and the team agreed upon common meanings and terminologies.

4 Grouping data together to produce themes

This stage is sometimes referred to as axial coding or as a separate stage. In this stage the coded data is placed into larger groups and synthesized to show how the topics that are produced interrelate. Critical factors are revealed which are then used to explain the themes that have emerged. It is vital that these factors naturally emerge and are not due to any other influences. Tentative propositions are then made regarding the relationships between the different themes that are produced. Attride-Stirling (2001) identified three levels of themes:

- basic: where the prominent messages and key premises are identified but are not yet linked;
- organizing: this involves clustering the themes to show how they interrelate to each other;
- global: this involves integrating the themes in order to show the global picture.

Exercise 6.4

Can you identify any themes from your own analysis of your colleague's text?

---

5 Creating theory

Again, this stage is sometimes described as a discrete stage and sometimes it is considered a form of selective coding. The creating theory stage places the themes in order to construct theory. Data is systematically selected and compared with existing models within the literature in order to construct explanations. Data is put into theoretical schemes until the best explanation is determined. The new theory is then applied to other populations and settings in order to establish the usefulness of the new theory. This allows the participants' perspectives to be analysed within the context of the world view.

Exercise 6.5

After using the five stages to analyse your text, what can you conclude about how people can make themselves unhealthy?

Types of analysis

The next section will discuss the four most common types of data analysis that are used in qualitative research. This will be followed by a discussion of some of the most useful models of analysis that are currently employed to analyse the different types of data and the chapter will conclude by examining some of the computer assisted programmes that exist to help code and categorize data.

Thematic analysis

Thematic analysis searches for common themes that emerge throughout a set of interviews; these are then built up into a theory to explain phenomena. As thematic analysis explores phenomena it is most commonly used in phenomenological studies. Text is analysed paragraph by paragraph. Data is broken down into codes, clustered into categories and then built up into themes which are used to describe the essence of the experience under investigation. Themes are threads of meaning that occur throughout the text; in other words they are concerned with what the text is talking about. They are the parts of the text that come together to address a particular topic. For example, a paragraph of text such as the one below could be presented:

> I think that health care is about thinking about people's problems and identifying the right care strategies for them, the strategies have to be culturally relevant and acceptable, for example, it's no good giving nicotine patches to every person who wants to stop smoking as they may suffer from rashes or may not like the appearance of very visible patches stuck on their arms or legs. The other thing is that the patches actually have to work and for some people they aren't all that effective, they sometimes need other aids such as inhalators or gum.

The first stage of thematic analysis would be to identify codes that relate to health care. The codes that could be identified from the above paragraph could be:

1   a thinking activity;
2   problems;
3   people centred;
4   culturally relevant;
5   smoking cessation help is an activity for healthcare professionals;
6   people can suffer from side effects;
7   interventions need to work;
8   interventions are not always effective;
9   multiple therapies may be needed;
10   strategies.

The codes with similar words or relationships would then be clustered into groups. For example:

•   Cluster one: a thinking activity, problems and strategies
•   Cluster two: people centred, culturally relevant, side effects, need to work
•   Cluster three: interventions, smoking cessation, multiple therapies

The clusters could then be used to produce three themes:

1   the nature of health care;
2   the acceptability of health care;
3   activities performed for health care.

These three themes could then be used to describe the essence of health care as a subjective phenomenon that involves carrying out activities that may not always be acceptable to all people but has at its heart a problem-solving approach. This theory could then be compared with existing theories and transferred into the real world to enhance understanding.

A number of authors have used thematic analysis to explore health care; for example, Jinks (1997) used thematic analysis to investigate caring in relation to student centred teaching while Ross (2000) found it to be very useful when investigating the experiences of carers of terminally ill patients. Ross (2000) used thematic analysis to explore the origins of caring and identified six themes:

•   affective dimensions of caring that involved feelings and attitudes;
•   psychomotor dimensions that involved behaviours that are recognized as caring;
•   cultural aspects that related to caring as a learned endeavour;

- exposure which implied that caring has to be experienced to be recognized as caring;
- precarious ordering which implied that there are two levels of caring;
- competency which related to caring as fundamental to the healthcare role.

From the themes that were identified caring was acknowledged as a learned endeavour that could be taught through curriculum and modelled through behaviours. Ross used the identified themes to create a model of human caring that is used in nurse education in the UK. Crawford et al. (2008) used thematic analysis to explore how mental health nurses perceive their professional identity and identified four themes:

- the client perspective which involved the public's perception of mental health nurses as counsellors and altruistic listeners rather than high level professionals;
- not being a professional which involved the mental health nurses perceiving themselves as helpers;
- growing out of the role which involved mental health nurses trying to become more professional by undertaking extended roles and courses;
- waiting to be discovered which involves the mental health nurses perceiving themselves as professionals but waiting to be acknowledged.

In order to explain and rationalize the themes Crawford et al. used narratives from the participants and were very explicit in the need to use the exact words expressed by the participants. However, Parahoo (2006) states that themes are indications from the data, not explicit dictations and therefore require an element of researcher judgement. The researcher has to interact with the data and actively think about which codes and categories link together and why they are linked. To some extent this method is open to criticism concerning the issue of researcher bias as the researcher has to draw from a range of options and the themes can be subjectively selected. There is an assumption that there will be a fit between the product of the data analysis and some external reality. This implies that thematic analysis will show up what already exists rather than creating anything new and also raises the following question: is the meaning really present within the data or does the researcher impose meaning upon the data?

Bracketing

When using thematic analysis for phenomenological studies a decision must be made whether to bracket pre-existing knowledge as Husserl suggests or to accept the researcher as an instrument as Heidegger advocates. Both approaches are acceptable depending upon the philosophical approach adopted by the researcher. Parahoo (2006) argues that foreknowledge has the potential to unconsciously bias the research process which leads to the researcher not being as open to the participants' experiences. Physiotherapist lecturer, Hurst (2010), used bracketing when exploring how physiotherapists make the transition from physiotherapist to lecturer in higher education. Hurst stated that prior to analysis she reflected upon her own transitional experience in an effort to clear her mind and suspend any preconceptions. The Heideggarian approach is the most popular approach for healthcare researchers as Hamill and Sinclair (2010) acknowledge bracketing as very difficult to achieve. They add that healthcare professionals prefer to draw on existing knowledge and clinical practice in order to work collaboratively with participants. This appears to be more congruent with the principles of health care which are concerned with promoting strong relationships, trust and good communication.

In some ways thematic analysis mirrors real life as when we interpret phenomena we first break it down and ask what it is. We then debate how it fits with similar phenomena that we have experienced and lastly form a theory about its nature.

Content analysis

Content analysis is a method of analysing narratives or word responses and is commonly used in phenomenology, case studies or narratives. It is very useful for establishing patterns and trends and can be used to analyse any data that arises from communication. For example, content analysis is popular with the media and could be used to analyse the public's perceptions of popular health issues such as Philo's study (2006) that explored the public's attitudes towards patients suffering from schizophrenia. Philo was able to assess the attitudes held by the public through their frequent use of words such as 'barmy', 'neurotic' and 'psychopath'.

The aim of content analysis is to interpret meaning from the content of text, identify patterns in the text and place the responses into categories. In contrast to thematic analysis which examines the text paragraph by paragraph, content analysis examines the whole transcript and selects topics or categories as units of meaning. There are approximately 10 to 15 categories per study. Categories may be defined as groups of content that share some commonality. Categories that are too broad will be too difficult to manage while categories that are too narrow may lose their essential meaning and become sterile. The researcher continually places information into categories until they become saturated. The categories are then broken down into sub-categories so that a tree diagram emerges. Once saturated, the researcher writes descriptive paragraphs about each category and looks for relationships which can then be combined to produce theory.

Jackson (2009) states that content analysis precedes the introduction of qualitative research and was used as early as 1740 in Sweden to analyse the content of hymns that were perceived as containing sinful content. Content was placed into five categories:

- sinful
- non-sinful
- favourable
- non-favourable
- neutral.

The analysis of the content resulted in some words in the hymns being changed to accommodate the demands of the new church congregation. Both Jackson's work and Philo's work highlight one of the major strengths of content analysis; that is, the capacity to transfer words into numbers in order to analyse data both qualitatively and quantitatively, thereby enriching the wholeness of the study. The qualitative data can also be used to generate hypotheses which can be tested to produce new theory. The major drawback to using content analysis is the inability to determine why events occur as content analysis can only highlight existing data; it cannot highlight the motivations behind the phenomena.

Constant comparative

The constant comparative method is used to analyse data generated from grounded theory. Mok et al. (2010) used the constant comparative method when exploring healthcare professionals' perceptions of distress in patients with advanced cancer. They sampled the experiences of physicians, nurses, social workers, occupational therapists, physiotherapists and chaplains. Open, axial and selective coding were used as recommended by Straus and Corbin (1998). The codes and categories led to the identification of three causal conditions of existential distress which could be considered to change practice.

As the title suggests, the key feature of the constant comparative method is the constant comparison of data in order to decide whether the identified themes fit to form theory. Data collection and analysis occur simultaneously and each transcript is compared and contrasted to highlight their similarities and differences. This means that after coding the first transcript, each subsequent transcript is systematically searched for similar or contrasting data and new codes are created as necessary. For example, the researcher will ask questions such as 'how is this person's experience similar to the previous person's experience?' or 'what are the differences between each of the three participants' experiences?'.

A key feature of grounded theory is the use of theoretical sampling where the researcher samples until the data becomes saturated and no new codes emerge. Once this stage is achieved data collection and analysis ceases and theory is generated from the codes and categories that have emerged. Analysis only ceases when:

- no new information emerges despite increasing the sample size;
- each category has been sufficiently described in terms of its characteristics and processes;
- links between categories have been established.

In grounded theory there is usually a core category that recurs through every other category and tends to provide the essence of the experience forming the basis of the theory. Mok et al. (2010) identified existential distress as their core category and described this as feeling lost, struggling and finding no reason to carry on living. At the end of the study the theory is compared and contrasted with existing theory through a literature review in order to validate the emerging theory and themes. Glaser (1992) argues that an initial literature review could contaminate the data and impose theory rather than allowing it to generate naturally.

Exercise 6.6

Can you identify any differences between thematic analysis and the constant comparative method? Some suggestions are provided in the Appendix.
Read this article:

> Hewitt-Taylor, J. (2001) Use of constant comparative analysis in qualitative research, *Nursing Standard*, 15(42): 39–42.

The article describes a study that used the constant comparative method of analysis to explore self-directed learning in paediatric nurse education. The study is written in a simple way and describes each stage of the analysis in a reader-friendly way.

Models of analysis

Several models of data analysis have been used in qualitative research. The most commonly used are: Colaizzi (1978), Van Kaam (1966) and Giorgi (1970). Each model will now be discussed.

Colaizzi

Colaizzi (1978) is the model most frequently used to analyse data from phenomenological studies; for example, Herth (1998) used Colaizzi to investigate the concept of hope in homeless children. Sixty homeless children were asked to describe their understanding of hope through drawings. This stage was followed by semi-structured interviews where each child was asked to discuss their drawings. Both the drawings and transcripts were analysed using Colaizzi's framework. Herth claimed that the real essence of hope came alive through the analysis of the drawings and stories and confirmed that despite their dire circumstances the majority of children were able to envisage a positive future. This study was important for developing further hope-fostering strategies that could be used in a variety of settings. McGivern (2009) used Colaizzi to explore coaching professionals' experiences of supervision and found that the validation process made participants feel involved and valued. Colaizzi's (1978) model has seven stages of analysis:

1   Read all of the subject's descriptions in order to get an overall feeling for them.
2   Identify specific statements that relate to the phenomena being studied – this stage equates with the descriptive stage advocated by some researchers.
3   Look for the meanings within the statements – this stage equates with coding in other models of analysis.
4   Organize the meanings into themes and validate them against the original statements. This stage involves identifying common experiences and clustering them.
5   Integrate the findings into an exhaustive description of the phenomena being studied. The themes are compared and contrasted and a theoretical model to describe the phenomena is formulated.
6   The findings are validated with the original participants.
7   Any changes offered by the participants are used to form a conclusive understanding of the phenomena. A new model is constructed that reflects the essential structures of the phenomena. Swanson-Kauffman and Schonwald (1988) refer to this model as a skeleton that can be filled with the rich story of each informant. The construction of a theoretical model implies that there is the potential for generalizability as each person fits their individual experience into a universal framework.

Van Kaam

Van Kaam (1966) is one of the older models of analysis and focuses on the frequency that phenomena occur at. The strength of Van Kaam's model is the process of expert validation that is adopted. A panel of expert judges is used to validate each stage of the analysis, which consists of six stages:

1   Expressions are listed and grouped. Groups are then validated by expert judges and presented as percentages.
2   Terms are reduced and refined into precise descriptions and once again are validated by expert judges.
3   Elimination of irrelevant data is carried out.
4   A raw description of the phenomena is established
5   The description is applied to randomly selected participants for validation.
6   The description of the phenomena is accepted as a valid reality.

Giorgi

Giorgi (1985) differs from Colaizzi and Van Kaam in that there is no method of validation: the analysis relies soley on the intuitive judgement of the researcher. Giorgi's model has been used by Baker (2010) to investigate how midwives give emotional support to pregnant women and by Woodman and Radzyminski (2009) to explore women's perceptions of life following breast reduction. Occupational therapists Forhan et al. (2010) used Giorgi's model to explore the lived experiences of people with obesity. Giorgi advocates a four-stage process:

1   The researcher reads every transcript to get a feeling for the context and emotions as a whole.
2   The researcher re-reads each transcript individually and identifies codes and themes. For example, Forhan et al. identified sections in the text that related to how obese people are able to contribute in daily occupations and identified three themes: tensions, barriers and strategies.
3   The researcher looks for relationships within the themes in order to make sense of the whole. In Forhan et al.'s study the descriptions given by the participants were transformed into language used by occupational therapists in order to make the findings discipline specific and add relevancy. For example, the phrase 'tying shoes' was replaced by 'dressing lower extremity'.

4   The researcher synthesizes all of the themes into a consistent statement that reflects the essence of the participant's experiences. Forhan et al. concluded that the physical consequences of living with obesity limits participations in some aspects of everyday living; however, occupational therapy has the potential to strengthen these clients' potential by addressing barriers that exist in the social environment.

There are many other models of analysis that are used in qualitative research such as Benner (1984) who advocates three stages, Burnard (1991) who advocates 14 stages and Cormack (2000) who has a model with five stages. Regardless of the model that is adopted, the process of analysis is time-consuming and involves sticking and pasting using lots of multicoloured paper. In an attempt to reduce the process and speed up the coding and categorizing several computer assisted software packages have been developed. These will be discussed in the next section.

Computer assisted techniques

Computer assisted qualitative data software (CAQDAS) has been acknowledged as helpful to modern researchers as manual data analysis has been described as overwhelming and time-consuming (Parahoo 2006). Computer assisted techniques can speed up the process of analysis and have the potential to simplify procedures. Many researchers have commented that computer assisted software is unobtrusive and acknowledge that there is less potential for biases that result from the subjective judgements of the researcher. Webb (1999) identifies that there is the potential for researchers to over-use mechanical processes which can result in lost creativity and 'getting lost in hyperspace'. She adds that the researcher is alienated from the data, which results in the loss of valuable context. Another criticism made by Webb (1999) concerns the extent to which the coding process isolates words from the context in which they occur; this results in words becoming sterile with some of the meaning getting lost or fragmented. Webb likens this process to doing a jigsaw puzzle without a picture. However, some researchers praise the extent of the indexing systems that exist in computer aided packages and find them particularly useful when comparing and contrasting the importance of issues that arise from the text. A wide variety of packages exist but many of them possess the same functions. These include the ability to:

- store and retrieve text;
- find words, phrases or segments of data;
- label data;

- sort and organize data into manageable sections;
- prepare diagrams.

This next section will identify some of the computer assisted software used most frequently for analysing qualitative data. The aim of this section is not to demonstrate how to use software packages but to inform the reader about what exists.

NUD.IST (NVivo)

NUD.IST stands for Non-numerical Unstructured Data Indexing and is the leading package used for content analysis but has been renamed NVivo. To date there are six different version of NUD.IST in operation. NUD.IST will search the content for codes (closely correlating words) to create patterns or categories that can be used to form associations of ideas. NUD.IST is most often used for the analysis of data used in grounded theory; for example, Chiang (2008) used it in his grounded theory study of critically ill patients. He describes NUD.IST as having powerful data management capacity that enhanced the effectiveness and efficiency of his analysis. Darrow et al. (2001) also used NUD.IST to analyse very large volumes of data from their study that explored the information needs of prostate cancer sufferers in the USA. They used telephone narratives to gain data from 536 patients and 436 significant others. The researchers found that their analysis would have been impossible without the use of computer assisted software due to the large sample size. NUD.IST has the advantage of being able to identify codes that could be missed or not recognized through manual analysis. However, there are some restrictions concerning the size of the words, sentences and paragraphs that can be analysed. Data from video and photographs can also be analysed with text. This package has the advantage of being available in multiple languages and can graphically display models, charts and tables. Modern versions of NVivo will also allow separate research projects to be combined for broader analysis.

Ethnograph

Ethnograph codes information and searches for occurrences of the codes across different groups. For example, Pontin (1977) used the Ethnograph to compare qualitative data from nursing staff and patients when investigating the use of primary nursing. Using the Ethnograph enabled Pontin to easily identify common themes and to code data far more rapidly than when using manual methods. There are some restrictions regarding how data needs to be presented; for example, the text is limited to no more than 40 characters wide.

However, the advantage for students is the useful tutorial that accompanies the software for ease of use.

ATLAS.ti

This is software designed to assist in text analysis and model building. It is sophisticated in that it can work with text, audio, graphs and video data. It will select and code segments of text and display any existing relationships and patterns. Web pages to share with collaborators can also be developed. For researchers using mixed-method approaches data can even be linked to SPSS for statistical analysis. It is described as particularly good at identifying hidden phenomena. Further information on ATLAS.ti can be found at the ATLAS.ti website (http://www.atlasti.com).

TextSmart

TextSmart is part of SPSS and is used to code and categorize words used in open-ended surveys. It clusters terms and responses to create meaningful categories. The researcher can change the parameters to create their own categories in order to feel more involved in the analysis.

Qualrus

This package is very user friendly and is designed to assist with coding data. However, many researchers describe it as slow with large amounts of data but very efficient with average amounts of data as it uses simple language and has a quick learning curve.To assist students a free downloadable demo is available (http://www.qualrus.com).

The General Inquirer

The General Inquirer was developed at Harvard in the 1960s and is one of the most commonly used content analysis packages used in the USA but it is not as popular in the United Kingdom. It contains large content dictionaries that recognize most words used in modern-day language and combines these with text scanning software to search for patterns and meanings in sentences.

Advantage and disadvantages

This section has discussed the potential usefulness of computer assisted software packages that are available for analysing qualitative data. The advantages that relate to speediness and ease of coding have been highlighted and the numerous packages that can assist in this process have been identified. However, it has been argued that computer assisted methods have the potential to fragment data and reduce creativity through their reductionist approach to data. The decision regarding the use of computer packages has to be made according to the needs of the study. For example, if a large sample has been used resulting in a vast amount of data to be analysed, using a computer aided package may be useful. Alternatively, if the data to be analysed is relatively small and easy to manage using a manual approach is preferred as the researcher is able to familiarize themselves with the data and retain the artistry that is inherent in the qualitative approach. While software packages can be useful resources it is important to consider that their role is to manage data not to analyse it. The analysis remains under the control of the researcher and sound judgements are still required regarding the nature of the text. Computers are not a substitute for thinking.

Exercise 6.7

Read the following article. It gives a very simplistic overview of the advantages and disadvantages of using computer assisted software.

McLafferty, E. and Farley, A.H. (2006) Analysing qualitative research data using computer software, *Nursing times.net*, 102(24): 34–5.

Summary

This chapter has discussed the process of qualitative analysis. Seven key stages have been identified that appear to feature in most models and theories. The seven stages have been discussed and linked to health care in order to highlight their relevance. Three main methods of analysis have been compared and contrasted: content analysis and thematic analysis have been described as useful to phenomenology and narrative research while the constant comparative method has been linked to grounded theory. Each method has been described as labour intensive and laborious so computer assisted software has been offered as a quicker method of coding and categorizing data. The most commonly used software packages have been discussed. However, computer assisted technology has been accused of fragmenting data and isolating the researcher from the interpretive process. The techniques and tools that are selected need to be evaluated according to the skills of the researcher, the nature of the research and the resources that are available. Qualitative research remains an interpretive process and regardless of the tools that are used the judgements and interpretations of the researcher will always be crucial to the process.

Jargon busting

Make a list of any words in this chapter that you do not understand. Look up their meaning and consider their use in the world of research. You may identify some of the following words and terms:

Analysis: Establishing meaning from the data that is produced.
Coding: The process of identifying important words or phases that can be placed into categories or transformed into symbols than can be computerized.
Constant comparative: The method of analysis used in grounded theory. The researcher continuously compares data as it is acquired.
Content analyisis: A method of analysis used in narratives and phenomenology.
Saturation: The point where data collection ceases in grounded theory. No more theory is developed as the data becomes repetitive.
Skype: Software that enables people to make videos, converse online through the internet and share files for business, research or personal purposes.
Theme: Labelling data according to similarities that are found.
Theoretical sampling: The sampling method used for grounded theory. The researcher samples until no new data occurs. The data is then considered to be saturated.
Transcript: A written testimony of a participant's interview.
Validity: The extent to which an instrument or method measures what it claims to be measuring.
Verbatim: The process of transcribing an interview where every word is written exactly as it is spoken.

References

Attride-Stirling, J. (2001) Thematic networks: an analytic tool for qualitative research, *Qualitative Research*, 1(3): 385–405.
Baker, S. (2010) How do midwives emotionally support women becoming mothers? A phenomenological study. Unpublished PhD thesis, Bournemouth University.
Benner, P. (1984) *From Novice to Expert: Excellence and Power in Clinical Practice*. Menlo Park, CA: Addison-Wesley.

Bowling, A. (2009) *Research Methods in Health: Investigating Health and Health Services*. Maidenhead: Open University Press.

Burnard, P. (1991) A method of analysing interview transcripts in qualitative research, *Nurse Education Today*, 11: 461–6.

Chiang, V. (2008) *The use of N4 in a grounded theory study*. http://www.nursing.bcs.org/itin17/chiang.htm. (accessed 5 November 2010).

Colaizzi, P.F. (1978) Psychological research as the phenomenologist views it, in: R.S. Valle and M. King (eds) *Existential Phenomenological Alternatives for Psychology*. New York: Oxford University Press.

Cormack, D.F. (2000) *The Research Process in Nursing*. Oxford: Blackwell Science.

Crawford, P., Brown, B. and Mojomi, P. (2008) Professional identity in community mental health nursing: a thematic analysis, *International Journal of Nursing Studies*, 45: 1055–63.

Darrow, S.L., Kawasumi, Y., Levine, S.A. and Hayes, D. (2001) Cancer information seekers. Patients and significant others. Paper presented at the International Social Technological Assessment of Health Care Meeting.

Forhan, M., Law, M.C., Vrkljan, B.H. and Taylor, V.H. (2010) The experience of participation in everyday occupations for adults with obesity, *Canadian Journal of Occupational Therapy*, 77(4): 210–17.

Giorgi, A. (1970) *Psychology as a Human Science*. New York: Harper and Row.

Giorgi, A. (1985) *Phenomenology and Psychological Research*. Pittsburgh: Duquesne University Press.

Glaser, B.G. (1992) *Basics of Grounded Theory Analysis*. Mill Valley: Sociology Press.

Hamill, C. and Sinclair, H. (2010) Bracketing – practical considerations in Husserlian phenomenological research, *Nurse Researcher*, 17(2): 17–24.

Herth, K. (1998) Hope as seen through the eyes of homeless children, *Journal of Advanced Nursing*, 28(5): 1053–62.

Hurst, K.M. (2010) Experiences of new physiotherapy lecturers making the shift from clinical practice into academia, *Physiotherapy*, 96: 240–7.

Jackson, M. (2009) Content analysis, in: J. Neale (ed.) *Research Methods for Health and Social Care*. Basingstoke: Palgrave Macmillan.

Jinks, A. (1997) *Caring for Patients, Caring for Student Nurses: Developments in Nursing and Healthcare*. Aldershot: Ashgate.

McGivern, L. (2009) Continuous professional development and avoiding the vanity trap. An exploration of coaches' experiences of supervision, *International Journal of Evidence Based Coaching and Mentoring*, 3: 22–5.

Mok, E., Lau, K., Chan, L., Jeffrey, S.C. and Chan, K. (2010) Healthcare professionals' perceptions of existential distress in patients with advanced cancer, *Journal of Advanced Nursing*, 66(7): 1510–22.

Moule, P., Albarran, J., Bessant, E., Pollock, J. and Brownfield, C. (2008) A comparison of e-learning and classroom delivery of basic life support with automated external defibrillator use: a pilot study, *International Journal of Nursing Practice*, 14: 427–34.

Orpen, N. and Harris, J. (2010) Patients perceptions of home-based occupational therapy and/or physiotherapy interventions prior to total hip replacements, *British Journal of Occupational Therapy*, 73(10): 461–9.

Parahoo, K. (2006) *Nursing Research: Principles, process and issues.* Basingstoke: Palgrave Macmillan.

Philo, G. (2006) *Media and Mental Distress.* London: Longman.

Pontin, D. (1977) Primary nursing: a mode of care or a nursing philosophy, *Clinics of North America*, 2(4): 751–62.

Ross, T. (2000) *A phenomenological study exploring perceptions of caring.* Unpublished dissertation.

Straus, A. and Corbin, J. (1998) *Basics of Qualitative Research: Grounded Theory Procedures and Techniques.* California: Sage.

Swanson-Kauffman, K.M. and Schonwald, E. (1988) Phenomenology, in: B. Sarter (ed.) *Paths to knowledge: Innovative Research Methods for Nursing.* New York: National League for Nursing.

Van Kaam, A. (1966) *Existential Foundations of Psychology.* Pittsburgh: Duquesne University Press.

Webb, C. (1999) Analysing qualitative data: computerised and other approaches, *Journal of Advanced Nursing*, 29(2): 323–30.

Woodman, R. and Radzyminski, S. (2009) Women's perceptions of life following breast reduction, *Plastic Surgical Nursing*, 29(1): 39–46.

7 Mixed methods

Introduction

> If the only tool researchers have is a hammer, they tend to see every problem as a nail (Stange and Zyzanski 1989: 4)

This quote by Stange and Zyzanski implies that if researchers practise ritualistically using only one approach, they may never broaden their horizons to perceive the world from more than one perspective and may never actually discover anything new. The previous four chapters have explored quantitative and qualitative research and each approach has been identified as having strengths and weaknesses. For example, quantitative studies have high reliability but low validity whereas qualitative studies have their strength in their validity but cannot be replicated or generalized to the wider population.

There are very strong arguments for combining approaches in order to capitalize on the strengths and produce a more holistic view of the phenomena being investigated. Several researchers refer to mixed methods as the third paradigm (Burke Johnson and Onwuegbuzie 2004; Giddings 2006) and argue that combining approaches offers the best of both worlds. Borkan (2004) claims that mixing methods expands the researcher's toolbox. This chapter will explore the rationales for combining research approaches, identify ways in which approaches can be used in a complementary manner and critically debate the arguments for and against mixing methods.

Learning outcomes

At the end of this chapter you will be able to:

- define the term mixed methods;
- discuss the rationales for mixing research approaches;

- identify the types of triangulated approaches that are used in health-care research;
- debate the strengths and weaknesses of triangulated approaches.

What are mixed methods?

We mix methods in many of our daily activities; for example, if we want to get to a new venue, town or city that we haven't been to before we might use a satellite navigation system to guide us. However, these have been known to guide people off the edges of cliffs and down one way streets – hence we may also use an up-to-date map as a backup. Alternatively, if we are shopping we may pay for some items using a credit card but to only carry a credit card may limit the items that we are able to purchase as not all shops are able to use them, so sometimes we also have to purchase goods with cash. If we are purchasing a pack of butter, one brand may be very cheap but tasteless; therefore we evaluate the purchase in terms of the quantitative (price) and the qualitative (taste and texture). Sometimes selecting one method to achieve an aim can be very limiting and it is more realistic to mix approaches. The same principles can be applied if we consider the issue of research.

A number of terms are used interchangeably in the literature when referring to combining approaches; for example, mixed methods, triangulation, method slurring and multi-method are most commonly used. Triangulation is usually used to describe a study that blends elements of quantitative and qualitative paradigms. Several different types of triangulation have been identified:

- *Investigator triangulation* is the process of using two investigators with divergent backgrounds to explore the same phenomenon. For example, Kennedy (2004) used the Delphi technique which involves surveying the views of experts. He used two different panels to examine midwifery processes from two different perspectives and he followed this up with narrative interviews and concluded that the narratives confirmed the findings from the Delphi survey and produced a more robust description of midwifery practices.
- *Data triangulation* is the collection of data from multiple sources for the same study. The aim is to obtain diverse views about the phenomena in order to validate its state. An example of data triangulation could be if midwives wanted to know whether breastfeeding or bottle feeding was the most effective method of satisfying a baby's need for food. The midwives would sample mothers from several different countries who used different methods of feeding. Alternatively if a researcher wanted to investigate how healthcare professionals

perceive health, he may sample nurses, physiotherapists, chiropractors, doctors, dieticians and radiographers.

- *Analysis triangulation* is where different types of analysis are applied to the same set of data. Onwuegbuzie and Leech (2004) used mixed analysis to establish a link between three types of anxiety and the scores that undergraduate students attained for their research proposals. Quantitative statistics were applied to the results of three types of anxiety scales: a library anxiety scale, a statistics anxiety scale and a composition anxiety scale. The students' reflexive journals were analysed qualitatively using constant comparison. The results concluded that the students with the highest levels of anxiety reported behaviours that affected their abilities to construct a research proposal indicating that there was a strong relationship between anxieties and writing research proposals. Onwuegbuzie and Leech stated that analysis triangulation enriched their understanding of the role that anxiety plays in educational ability. In contrast, Savage (2000) found that using two different forms of analysis on the same text produced very diverse and incompatible interpretations.
- *Methods-based triangulation* is the use of two or more research methods in a single study such as Drennan's (2002) into the role of the clinical placement coordinator. Drennan used focus groups, individual interviews and questionnaires to establish the usefulness of the placement coordinator role. Howard and Kneafsey (2005) also used focus groups, interviews and questionnaires to explore the impact of research governance. Researchers can use methods from the same paradigm such as a survey and an experiment or an observation and interviews or they can mix paradigms such as using semi-structured interviews and a randomized control trial.
- *Theoretical triangulation* involves blending diverse theories in order to apply different philosophical viewpoints to the same phenomena. For example, television and radio presenters who are exploring an issue will often select two speakers with very diverse views in order to make a programme more interesting.

Exercise 7.1

Identify the method(s) of triangulation that has/have been used in the following study. The answer is in the Appendix.

Burdett (2000) conducted a comparison study of women's perceptions of satisfaction and participation using an Electronic Meeting System compared to a

(continued)

conventional meeting format. Thirty women provided feedback via a question-naire that was analysed using a coefficient. In addition Burdett used observations from her experience as a meeting facilitator and semi-structured interviews that were analysed using thematic analysis. More women were satisfied with Electronic Meeting Systems than with conventional meetings.

Figure 7.1 demonstrates that research occurs in stages but the process is cyclical in that at the start the researcher considers whether a mixed method approach can best answer the research question and reflectively reconsiders this issue at the end of the research. For this reason the stages have not been numbered. We can see that mixing methods can occur at any stage in the research process. The important consideration is why the research should be mixed and what is the added value?

Rationales for mixing methods

Several rationales exist for mixing methods: some researchers argue that mixing methods can provide a more holistic view of healthcare problems and offer

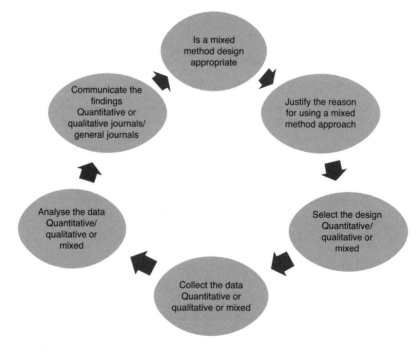

Figure 7.1 Stages in the mixed method process.

a broader understanding of issues compared to mono approaches while some researchers suggest that mixing methods adds to the reliability and validity of findings in order to discover whether different approaches produce similar results. Some researchers argue that mixing methods prevents paradigm wars where researchers are constrained by the rigid rules of one paradigm; combining approaches creates innovation and allows researchers more control in their methods. Each of these views will be examined in more detail.

The healthcare perspective

Blending quantitative and qualitative data is a commonly used approach in everyday health care; for example, when we assess patients we obtain subjective data about the patients' social background, family history, past medical history and daily patterns of living. We also acquire objective data such as blood pressure, pulse, blood tests, scans and others. We then combine the subjective and objective data in order to produce a differential diagnosis that can be used to plan healthcare interventions. Combining objective and subjective data enables us to view the patient holistically. Understanding patients holistically involves analysing the patient in terms of their biological, social, psychological and spiritual dimensions. Health care is complex; the importance of establishing cause and effect and disease statistics are crucial to developing cure strategies but understanding the patient experience can enrich the potential for cure and contribute to the promotion of effectiveness and efficiency. Furthermore, health care is concerned with multidisciplinary working where multiple perspectives and practices are used in synergy to help patients; if this is the reality for health care should this not be a reality for research too?

Exercise 7.2

Identify the ways that you use mixed method approaches in your everyday role.

Can you identify any advantages to using different approaches to get the job done?

Can you identity any problems or barriers to using multiple approaches?

Most discussions about mixed methods are linked to debates regarding the primacy of the two research paradigms or as Robson (2002) puts it 'the paradigm wars'. The debate as to which paradigm is superior, quantitative or qualitative has been prominent in the literature for many years and no conclusions have been drawn. The approach adopted is determined by the question that needs to be answered and for health care sometimes neither approach can singularly answer the research question or solve healthcare problems.

Muncey (2005) claims that the mixed method movement was originally an attempt to break down the divide between quantitative and qualitative research traditions or as she puts it 'to provide a bridge over troubled waters'. Giddings (2006) argues that a cooperative framework has the potential to move the debate beyond methodological competitiveness to a collective approach to dealing with health and social problems that cannot be solved by a mono-research design. She claims that a mixed method approach offers a bridge between paradigms offering researchers the opportunity to become more creative in their response to real health and social problems.

Giddings (2006) argues that there are four popular rationales for using a mixed method approach:

- the opportunity to be more holistic;
- to offer a broader understanding;
- to gain more certainty in the results;
- to enhance flexibility.

We will explore each of these in turn below.

Enhancing the holistic perspective

Enhancing the holistic perspective involves understanding the phenomena from more than one viewpoint. For example, a randomized control trial could produce statistics to show that larval therapy will enhance the debridement of wounds but does not demonstrate that patients will find larval therapy acceptable. Following up the statistics with interviews can evaluate the acceptability of this treatment and has the potential to reduce wasting resources if the majority of patients find it unacceptable. Borkan (2004) states that using one method allows the researcher to see only what you are looking at but mixing methods expands the gaze to notice elements that have never been previously considered.

Offering a broader understanding

Offering a broader understanding involves gaining insights that may not be available through the use of one approach. McEvoy and Richards (2006) refer to this process as achieving completeness. For example, a researcher may wish to explore how people feel about a new healthcare initiative such as eradicating sugar from coffee machines in NHS hospitals but in order to understand the views obtained, the researcher may need to interpret the views in terms of the demographics of the population who have been sampled. Many of those people sampled could be pre-diabetic and have been sugar users for many years while some people could be previously obese patients who have adopted new patterns of thinking and behaviours. The use of descriptive statistics can add understanding to the views obtained. Byng (2002) combined a randomized control trial with interviews in his study of people with long-term mental illness and commented that while mixing methods did not provide all of the answers that he was seeking, it helped him to develop a much deeper understanding of how and why improvements in care processes occurred.

Obtaining more certainty in the results

Triangulation can be used to enhance reliability by using two or more methods to address the same question or evaluate the validity of a tool; for example, a researcher may use focus groups in order to validate the use of a questionnaire. Drennan (2002) used the data from his focus groups and interviews to formulate a questionnaire that was used on a sample of 620 student nurses when he investigated the role of the clinical placement coordinator. If both methods produce similar findings the researcher will have more confidence in the use of the question or tool. Parahoo (2006) refers to this process as 'complementarity'. Parahoo argues that this form of triangulation is advantageous when there is consistency but problems arise when divergent data emerges. Mixing methods can be used to reduce sampling bias. For example, using one method of sampling such as convenience sampling may lead to the accidental exclusion of some client groups impairing the generalizability of the results; using face-to-face interviews with selected groups can add detail and enhance the quality of the study.

Enhancing flexibility

Triangulation has the potential to add flexibility and creativity to a study when the opportunity for further exploration occurs or the opportunity to change direction occurs due to unexpected findings. For example, Schillaci et al. (2004) were quantitatively investigating the use of Medicaid managed care in children living in New Mexico and noticed a sudden decrease in the uptake of immunizations. The research team responded by performing ethnographic research in order to explain the decrease in immunization rates. This increased flexibility allows researchers the opportunity to explore issues and opportunities as they occur and can provide the starting point for redirection.

The disadvantages of mixing methods

This chapter has discussed the many advantages of using mixed method approaches but despite the extensive literature that exists that claims to use mixed methods, significant challenges remain. The question as to whether paradigms should be combined has been a source of controversy in the literature and Borkan argues that despite the many advantages of mixing methods, numerous roadblocks exist. Hess-biber (2010) claims that a gold-rush mentality has resulted in many researchers using mixed method approaches too readily without adequate consideration and preparation. Hess-biber highlights that a *methods–experience gap* exists that impacts the credibility of mixed methods research; she states that using a mixed method approach requires knowledge and skill in several research approaches but most researchers tend to have expertise in one particular area.

Skills and understanding

Mixing methods involves researchers having to step outside of their comfort zones and experiment blindly. Trying to apply techniques without adequate training and understanding can damage the integrity of the research and limit the applicability of the findings. Mixing methods is expensive in terms of additional funding for resources and funding to train researchers as there is twice as much to learn. Hess-biber refers to mixed methods as taking a journey without being in control of your destination; by this she implies that when you experiment you never actually know what the end results will be.

To some extent mixing methods is high risk as the outcomes are harder to predict. However, other researchers would argue that it is the journey not the destination that matters as this is often where innovation presents itself.

Evaluating mixed method studies

Cresswell et al. (2004) identified the most common impediment to using mixed methods as lack of criteria to guide researchers in the practice of triangulation, which leads to many researchers adopting incompatible and meaningless research strategies with rationales that are not clearly articulated. Evaluating the quality of mixed approaches is problematic as universal criterion exists to evaluate both qualitative and quantitative research but none exists to evaluate mixed approaches and the criteria that currently exist are not appropriate. Brannen (2010) suggests that the criteria used should depend upon the dominance of the paradigm that is used and highlights that there is usually one paradigm that is more obvious. However, problems arise when both qualitative and quantitative elements appear to be present in equal proportions. Sim and Sharp (1998) add that there are not enough experts in the field of triangulation to direct and judge the processes that are used as the process is still emerging. Cresswell and Garrett (2008) refer to mixed methods as a 'movement' indicating that it is a growing trend rather than an established methodology and add that growing pains are a natural outcome.

Problems with publishing

As more researchers conduct mixed methods studies problems with publishing have arisen. Some journals favour particular research paradigms which results in researchers having to publish in several different journals. One solution has been to use a team approach where quantitative researchers perform and write about the quantitative results and the qualitative researchers perform and write up the qualitative findings. This results in readers only obtaining part of the information and questions the relevance of mixing the methods in the first place. The consequence of this approach is increased costs in terms of time to write different articles and having to pay multiple researchers. Cresswell (2003) claims that there are three perspectives that relate to mixing methods:

- *Purists* who oppose the mixing of methods in a single study. Purists argue that the methodology inherent to each study should be underpinned by a philosophical standpoint and each standpoint has mutually exclusive assumptions with no common ground. They argue that trying to mix incompatible theories leads to confusion and weak research findings. Assessing the rigour of triangulated studies is complicated as different criteria are applied to quantitative and qualitative studies. For example, combining Heideggarian phenomenology with quantitative research can produce problems as quantitative research is concerned with being detached and eliminating bias whereas Heidegger argues that bias is irrelevant as the researcher is part of the research process.

Exercise 7.3

Consider the two religions, Catholic and Hindu. Look up the key concepts within these two religions and consider in your own mind if there is any possibility of these two religions being combined in order to create a mixed philosophy religion. Are the major philosophical assumptions similar enough to combine or are they too diverse to consider mixing? Would there be any value to mixing religions or should they remain separated? This may seem a controversial issue as currently religions tend to be very segregated; however, research paradigms were also segregated until recently. This exercise should stimulate you to consider the realities of mixing diverse philosophies.

- *Situationalists* who believe that there are certain instances where it is appropriate to mix methods in a single study. Situationalists are also known in the literature as *anti-conflationists;* this group of researchers argue that the divide between qualitative and quantitative research is not as diverse as it is claimed and there is a lot of overlap. For example, post-positivism has some agreement with interpretivism in that they both argue that objectivity is not a realistic outcome. Situationalists would also agree that naturalism and positivism have some similarities as they both accept that there is a real world that exists and is there to be discovered. Situationalists accept that there is a case for mixing paradigms if the underpinning philosophies can be reconciled.

• *Pragmatists* are described as actively involved in using mixed methods in studies. Pragmatists argue that there are times when neither quantitative nor qualitative research can answer a question and therefore researchers should use whichever methods are most able to provide them with the required results. Pragmatists argue that combining methods can be complementary and is a more practical way of achieving healthcare outcomes.

Justification for mixing approaches

This chapter has shown that while mixing methods has its advantages concerns exist about the rationales for using combined approaches. The most critical issue for the integrity of a study lies in whether there is good justification for the approach chosen. The justification for using mixed methods should be based on:

• **The purpose of the study:** Cresswell et al. (2004) claim that a study is more robust when a rationale for triangulation is present; this justifies the approach and highlights the relevance of the types of methods that are used. For example, Baskerville et al. (2001) identified their rationale for triangulation when they studied practices for implementing guidelines in family practices in Ontario. They specified their rationale as 'to attain a complete understanding'. Kutner et al.'s (1999) rationale was to develop a new semi-structured survey instrument in their study into palliative care provision.

• **The consequences of the findings:** Crewes and Alexander's (1999) study produced findings that provided valuable insight into patterns of computer usage in five Far East universities. They combined open-ended interviews with a survey to produce data that could be applied to many other universities in order to enhance the effective use of information technology resources.

- **The potential audience for the study**: The multiple stakeholders within a particular study or organization may differ in what they want to learn from a project and adopting a mixed method approach can lead to the findings being sold to much wider audiences. Second, mixing methods can result in researchers re-examining their own ideas and philosophies in order to expand their personal world views and enrich their research practices. Researchers can be more open-minded and more receptive to innovations.
- **The expertise of the researcher or research team:** Using a mixed method approach is dependent upon the skills of the researcher(s) and these skills will determine the appropriateness of the design.

Summary

This chapter has discussed the advantages and disadvantages of combining research approaches. Mixed method research is referred to as the newest research paradigm or the third paradigm. Mixing methods offers researchers the flexibility of combining the strengths of some approaches while minimizing the weaknesses of others in order to produce more holistic and robust studies that can be communicated to wider audiences. The strengths of mixing approaches have been highlighted as: adding validity and reliability to weak studies, offering a broader understanding of healthcare issues and enhancing the creative potential of researchers. However, the logistics and rationality of combining approaches has highlighted a number of challenges for researchers. Mixing methods has been shown to be labour intensive as researchers need to be multi-skilled and flexible in their philosophical beliefs; learning new skills and changing patterns of thinking takes extra time and slows down the process. Using teams has been offered as a solution but this also has resource implications and may also result in fragmented findings.

Despite the challenges that have been identified, mixed method approaches appear to be gaining popularity and researchers appear to be developing more adventurous ways of thinking. Research approaches are continually evolving and need to evolve in response to the complex nature of health care. Brannen (2010) claims that using mixed methods research encourages researchers to think outside of the box and is a practice that should be welcomed.

Reflective activity

Consider the types of skills that researchers may need to produce a good piece of mixed methods research. If you were a researcher which types of research would you prefer to use: quantitative, qualitative or mixed approaches? Reflect upon the reasons why you have chosen this type of research.

Jargon busting

Make a list of any words in this chapter that you do not understand. Look up their meaning and consider their use in the world of research. You may identify some of the following words and terms:

Delphi technique: A form of surveying that uses the views of experts as data.

Holism: Having a wider world view is one interpretation. The term is also used in healthcare to consider patients in terms of their biological, social, psychological and spiritual backgrounds.

Mixed methods: The process of combining different approaches to reaching a goal.

Objective data: Information that is obtained through the use of instruments, i.e. blood pressure, temperature.

Pragmatic: Being sensible.

Research governance: The regulations and standards that exist to improve research quality in health and social care.

Subjective data: Information that is personal or unique to a particular person.

Triangulation: Combining different approaches in one study.

References

Baskerville, N.B., Hogg, W. and Lemelin, J. (2001) Process evaluation of a tailored multifaceted approach to changing family physician practices, *Family Practitioner*, 50: 242–9.

Borkan, J.M. (2004) Mixed methods studies: a foundation for primary care, *Annals of Family Medicine*, 2(1): 4–6.

Brannen, J. (2010) *Mixed Methods Research: A Discussion Paper.* London: National Centre for Research Methods.

Burke Johnson, R. and Onwuegbuzie, A.J. (2004) Mixed methods research: a research paradigm whose time has come, *Educational Researcher*, 33(7): 14–26.

Burns, N. and Grove, S.K. (2005) *The Practice of Nursing Research: Conduct, Critique and Utilization.* St Louis, MO: Elsevier Saunders.

Byng, R. (2002) Using the realistic evaluation framework to make a retrospective qualitative evaluation of a practice initiative. Paper presented at the *European Evaluation Society* biennial conference. Seville.

Cresswell, J.W. (2003) *Research Design: Quantitative and Qualitative Approaches.* Thousand Oaks, CA: Sage.

Cresswell, J.W., Fetters, M.D. and Ivankova, N.V. (2004) Designing a mixed methods study for primary care, *Annals of Family Medicine*, 2(1): 7–120.

Cresswell, J.W. and Garrett, A.L. (2008) The movement of mixed methods research and the role of educators, *South African Journal of Education*, 28: 321–33.

Crewes, T.B. and Alexander, M.W. (1999) Far eastern universities: a documentation of computer availability and funding, *Office Systems Research Journal*, 17(1): 29–36.

Drennan, J. (2002) An evaluation of the role of the clinical placement coordinator in student nurse support in the clinical area, *Journal of Advanced Nursing*, 40(4): 475–83.

Giddings, L.S. (2006) Mixed methods research, *Journal of Research for Nursing*, 11(3): 195–203.

Hess-biber, S.N. (2010) *Mixed Method Research: Merging Theory with Practice.* London: Sage.

Howard, M.L. and Kneafsey, R. (2005) The impact of research governance in healthcare and higher education institutions, *Journal of Advanced Nursing*, 49(6): 675–83.

Kennedy, H.P. (2004) Enhancing Delphi research: methods and results, *Journal of Advanced Nursing*, 45(5): 504–11.

Kutner, J.S., Steiner, J.F., Corbett, K.K., Jahnigen, D.W. and Barton, P.L. (1999) Information needs in terminal illness, *Social Science Medicine*, 48: 1341–52.

McEvoy, P. and Richards, D. (2006) A critical realist rationale for using a combination of quantitative and qualitative methods, *Journal of Research in Nursing*, 11(1): 66–78.

Muncey, T. (2005) Mixing art and science. A bridge over troubled water or a bridge too far? Presented at the *Mixed Methods in Health and Social Science* conference, Homerton School of Health Studies, Cambridge, UK.

Onwuegbuzie, A.J. (1997) Writing a research proposal: the role of library anxiety, statistics anxiety and composition anxiety, *Library and Information Science Research*, 19: 5–33.

Onwuegbuzie, A.J. and Leech, N.L. (2004) Enhancing the interpretation of significant findings: the role of mixed methods research, *The Qualitative Report*, 9(4): 770–5.

Parahoo, K. (2006) *Nursing Research: Principles, Process and Issues.* New York: Palgrave Macmillan.

Robson, C. (2002) *Real World Research.* Oxford: Blackwell.

Savage, J. (2000) One voice, different tunes; issues raised by dual analysis of a segment of qualitative data, *Journal of Advanced Nursing*, 31(6): 1493–500.

Schillaci, M.A., Waizkin, H. and Carson, E.A. (2004) Immunization coverage and Medicaid managed care in New Mexico: a multi-method assessment, *Annals of Family Medicine*, 2: 13–21.

Sim, J. and Sharp, K. (1998) A critical appraisal of the role of triangulation in nursing research, *International Journal of Nursing Studies*, 35: 23–31.

Stange, K.C. and Zyzanski, S.J. (1989) Integrating qualitative and quantitative research methods, *Family Medicine*, 21: 448–51.

8   Ethics in research

Introduction

Ethics define what is a right and wrong thing to do in society; as a minimum ethics help to guide notions of what is morally acceptable to a population and what is not acceptable. Research is a powerful activity in that the findings impact many facets of human life such as which drugs people can access, which policies will direct healthcare provision and the activities that count as health care. Healthcare research is perceived as beneficial for society as the outcomes improve quality and quantity of life. However, sometimes the research journey raises questions regarding what can be defined as acceptable practice; for example, cloning and stem cell research have advanced health science but are not acceptable to some members of society as their potential for producing a new race of 'super-beings' is a threat to normal society. This chapter will examine how ethical principles can be used to guide acceptable research practice.

Learning outcomes

At the end of this chapter you will be able to:

- discuss the relevance of ethics for researchers;
- identify the ethical principles that are used to guide the research process;
- identify strategies that are used in research to reduce the vulnerability of research participants;
- define the term research governance.

Why are ethics important to research?

Patients are vulnerable when they are ill as their physical and mental capacities may be impaired in some way, therefore they need protection. But research would not progress if only well people were accessed for studies. The challenge for the researcher is balancing the need to advance science against protecting the rights and dignity of vulnerable people. It could be argued that all research participants are in some way vulnerable as they lack the same level of research knowledge held by the researcher which puts them at a disadvantage. Questions such as: 'is there any potential for harm?' and 'who will have access to the data?' are sources of stress for research participants. Therefore, as a minimum every study should demonstrate that the researcher has considered all potential threats to vulnerability and has taken appropriate action where required. The problem for society concerns the fact that no absolute laws exist to define exactly what is morally right and wrong as ethical principles are informed by culture, religion and life experiences. If researchers were to practise according to their individual principles assuring the rights and dignity of participants would be impossible; therefore some universal ethical codes have been devised as a guide.

Ethical codes

Modern research has derived many of its ethical principles from the field of biomedical ethics which has at its heart the Hippocratic Oath. The Hippocratic Oath guides the practice of doctors and has three maxims:

- any actions must produce benefit for the patient;
- patient confidentiality must be preserved through the protection of data and privacy;
- professionalism and dedication must be adhered to, implying that doctors must not work to benefit their own self-interest and must be beyond corruption.

Nurses and Midwives also have the Code of Professional Conduct (Nursing and Midwifery Council 2008) that defines and dictates ethical practices. The Code of Professional Conduct highlights nurses' and midwives' accountability in the provision of high quality care and acts as a tool to safeguard the health and well being of vulnerable people. A breach of ethical principles may not necessarily lead to legal action in a court of law but healthcare professionals can be disciplined by their professional regulatory bodies.

Two further significant codes have guided ethical research: the Nuremberg Code and the Declaration of Helsinki. The Nuremberg code was published in 1947 in response to Nazi atrocities which included research studies performed on prisoners against their will and knowledge. The fundamental ethical principle that arose from this code was the principle of voluntary consent. Ten standards for ethical experimentation on humans were devised. These standards clearly explicated unacceptable research practices and circumstances. In 1964 the Nuremberg Code was amended to become the Declaration of Helsinki. This declaration added that ethical research should be performed by competent experts, reviewed by a committee of independent reviewers and should be scientifically justified. It was updated in 2000 and 2008 to include capacity to consent and consideration of vulnerability.

Exercise 8.1

Identify some instances and situations where you think that research participants could be vulnerable. For each situation that you identify write down how you think a researcher can alleviate or reduce the research participants' vulnerability.

Ethical principles

Undertaking research is justified by the pursuit of knowledge. We need to confidently predict healthcare outcomes and this involves performing research on humans. Many experiments have been performed on animals but there are arguments that the rights of animals should be protected; furthermore, Moule and Goodman (2009) highlight that animal testing does not provide strong enough evidence about the effects of drugs upon humans. As research has the potential for harm, consideration of ethical principles must be explicit in every study.

Beauchamp and Childress (1989) identified four principles that they claim must be upheld in any situation. They refer to these as the four *prima facie*, which is a legal term meaning 'on the face of it'. The four principles are:

- respect for autonomy
- justice
- beneficence
- non-maleficence.

Each of these four ethical principles will be discussed in depth.

Respect for autonomy

Respect for autonomy concerns the extent to which the researcher considers the decision-making capacity of research participants. Respecting autonomy involves offering participants the choice in whether to participate in research and respecting their decision not to participate or to withdraw without any prejudice or ill feeling. Participants can only be truly autonomous in their decisions if they are fully informed of all potential risks and benefits. The principle of veracity (truth-telling) is central to the integrity of every researcher as non-disclosure of information or telling untruths threatens the trusting relationship that is needed for the exchange of information. Crookes and Davies (2004) argue that sometimes selectively controlling information is justified as disclosing all of the known risks may induce anxiety for participants. For example, if we told patients every potential side effect of every drug nobody would ever use any medication. They suggest that a researcher should determine what it is reasonable for the participants to know in terms of acting in their best interests.

Sometimes researchers cannot disclose risks as they have not established them. For example, the purpose of a study may be to test a treatment in order to discover the side effects. Another example, which could be identified as immoral, is the process of giving placebos in randomized control trials as participants are to some extent being denied information regarding the exact nature of the intervention. However, complete disclosure in a randomized control trial could jeopardize the relevance of the study so Beauchamp and Childress (1989) suggest that disclosing the fact that there will be placebos given to some participants is acceptable practice. Ideally every participant should be given as much information as possible in order to make an informed decision and be given sufficient time to reflect upon the information.

Exercise 8.2

Reflect upon your own feelings about truth-telling and consider the following questions:

- Should people always tell the truth?
- Are there any instances where people should not tell the truth?
- If you were going to participate in a study what kinds of information would you want in order to make an informed decision?

There are no right and wrong answers to these questions but considering them may enhance your critical thinking skills when evaluating literature.

Capacity

The above section has considered the researchers role in giving information but autonomy is also concerned with ensuring that the information has been understood by the participants. Research is embroidered with jargon that many participants (and students) find difficult to disentangle. This jargon can be used unethically to highlight the benefits of a research study and to understate the risks. Sometimes jargon can be used quite innocently when giving information. It is easy for researchers to assume understanding on the part of participants as the researcher is familiar with research terms and cannot reasonably be expected to accurately assess the capacity of every respondent. However, as a minimum they should offer the opportunity for questioning and clarify any complex terminology.

Assessing a participant's capacity to understand information is difficult as reliable and valid tools for assessment do not exist. The Mental Capacity Act (Department of Health 2005) provides a statutory framework to empower and protect vulnerable people and states that capacity has to be assumed unless it is proven otherwise. The act sets out clear parameters for research practice and covers loss of capacity during a research project. The Mental Capacity Act (2005) states that despite their vulnerability, research can be carried out on those who lack capacity if:

- an ethics committee deems that it is safe;
- it is directly related to the person's condition;
- it cannot be performed on those who have capacity due to the condition or topic area;
- the research does not interfere with human rights;
- carers have been consulted.

Some groups of people may be more vulnerable than others when it comes to assessing capacity; vulnerable groups are identified as:

- children, particularly neonates but those with any hearing and speech impediments may also have higher vulnerability;
- ethnic minority groups especially if they have English as a second language;
- those with mental health problems;
- people with cognitive impairments or illnesses;
- people with identified or unidentified learning disabilities.

The Mental Capacity Act (2005) makes it clear that a person cannot be treated as unable to make decisions unless all practical steps to help the person have been exhausted. Enhancing understanding can be promoted through the use of information sheets; however, this assumes that every person has the capacity to read and that the language is suitable.

Assessing capacity is further constrained by the fact that capacity can be a temporary state that is impacted by stress and illness, therefore one-off

assessments can be meaningless and capacity should be re-evaluated throughout the study. For example, Hem et al. (2007) achieved consent from three
patients in a locked ward of an acute psychiatric institution in Norway. The
first patient felt that her experiences of psychosis would be useful to other sufferers and was very keen to participate. The following day the patient withdrew
claiming that the researcher was performing tests on her and was constantly
watching her moves. The second patient was excessively eager to participate
in the research and became obsessive to the extent that he wanted to direct
the research project. The third participant expressed interest in the research
and appeared to be knowledgeable but he developed an unhealthy interest in
the researcher and when this was not reciprocated he became verbally abu-
sive. Each of these instances demonstrated to Hem et al. that full consent 'is
an illusion' as capacity is so variable. The Mental Capacity Act (2005) was
amended in 2007 to become the Mental Health Act and new principles were
introduced to cover deprivation of liberty but issues regarding how to define
absolute capacity remain.

Exercise 8.3

Consider the following question and critically reflect upon your answer:

Should a person from a vulnerable group be denied participation in a research
study? If your answer is yes, what is your rationale? If your answer is no, how
could the person's vulnerability be minimized?

Confidentiality

Respecting the autonomy of participants also involves considering the need
for trust and confidentiality. Confidentiality is the right to privacy and respecting the participant's expectation not to be identified throughout the
research process. Qualitative research poses particular risks to confidentiality
as the process of description means that experiences are described in great
detail. This can result in some participants being identified by virtue of their
roles or by the detail provided in their responses. Confidentiality is linked to
anonymity, which is said to exist when the participant's identity cannot be
linked to the responses given and can be assured by assigning participants a
code number instead of using names or using pseudonyms. Confidentiality
assumes that the data provided by the participants will not be publicly di-
vulged and that it cannot be accessed by anyone other than the researcher.
This involves securing data in locked facilities and the stringent use of pass-
words. All data used in studies should be destroyed once the study has been

completed and firewalls should be in place. If confidentiality or anonymity cannot be protected participants should be informed at the beginning of the study before they agree to participate.

Justice

Justice is defined by Burns and Grove (2005) as the right to fair treatment. This implies that every person in a research study should be treated fairly and equally with respect for their individual rights. Participants should be selected according to their suitability for the study and not because they can be easily coerced. Examples of coercion include paying participants who may be vulnerable due to their financial status such as using students or targeting people in lower socio-economic groups. The most significant example of injustice in research occurred during the Second World War by Nazi doctors who performed experiments on prisoners in concentration camps. Another example of injustice in research is the Tuskegee Study into untreated syphilis in African-American males that took place in Alabama between 1932 and 1972. All of the participants were illiterate, very poor and did not give informed consent. They were offered free meals and medical insurance if they agreed to participate in the study. The aim of the study was to study the long-term effects of syphilis so most of the participants were given placebos rather than penicillin in order that the progressive effects of syphilis could be studied. From of a total of 399 subjects only 79 survived until the end of the study, most subjects dying from syphilis-related complications. Unfortunately the study also resulted in wives being affected by syphilis and children being born with congenital syphilis.

Most healthcare codes stress that healthcare professionals should offer impartial care and should not discriminate in any way; this includes offering equal care in terms of gender, age, religion and political beliefs. However, researchers and healthcare professionals exist in the world and as such form personal beliefs and attitudes. For example, Margalith et al. (2008) explored student nurses' care of terrorists and their victims in Israel. A total of 306 student nurses on a Bachelors nursing program were asked to give their responses to five vignettes where the patient was either a terrorist or a victim. When the patient was a terrorist in a life-threatening situation the nurses did not demonstrate any negative attitudes towards the patient but when the condition was non-life threatening the students were more likely to transfer their care to others or offer reduced care. This study demonstrated that student nurses found it difficult to comply with their professional codes of ethics which stressed the duty to offer equal care to every patient. In the interests of justice the interests of the participants should come before the objectives of the researcher.

Beneficence and non-maleficence

Beneficence refers to the extent that research should do good either for the participant or for society and non-maleficence is the extent to which harm has been prevented. The Declaration of Helsinki (World Medical Association 2008) stated that all research that involves humans should involve a careful assessment of all risks and benefits prior to being commenced. All research is potentially exploitive but it is the researchers' duty to prevent any foreseeable harm. However, harm is not always foreseeable or transparent. Parahoo (2006) points out that the participants in a study often receive new attention and when this is suddenly withdrawn participants can feel isolated and hurt. Richards and Schwarts (2002) stress that even qualitative research can induce painful memories or cause offence. Minimizing harm can be achieved by researchers critically reflecting upon the need for the research and upon their own skills as a researcher. Polgar (2008) claims that it is always researchers who have the most to gain from a study in terms of improved career prospects, raised professional esteem and satisfied curiosity. However, Hem et al. (2007) found that the researcher's knowledge of psychiatry helped her identify when participants were unable to consent due to impaired capacity. She was also able to sensitively withdraw from participants if she felt that her presence was a threat to the participant's mental health.

Ethical approval

As research impacts society and the decisions that people make it is important that all research is appropriate and designed to a high quality. All healthcare research proposals should be submitted to a body of reviewers called the ethics committee. An ethics committee consists of a panel of critics with an interest in research. A panel usually consists of academics, healthcare professionals, patients, lawyers, religious representatives and lay members of the public. The role of the ethics committee is to evaluate each research proposal for its scientific rigour, relevance to science and public safety. The ethics committee has to feel satisfied that the researcher has considered every possible action to safeguard the vulnerability of research participants. They insist that the researcher is clear about the nature of the research that the participants are entering into so that true informed consent can be assured. Additional functions of ethics committees include:

- evaluating the risks and benefits of a study;
- evaluating the skills of the researcher;
- assessing the feasibility of the study;
- assuring public confidence in the safety of research practice;

- identifying biases in a study with regards to sampling and funding;
- assuring the value of the research for the good of society;
- providing a mechanism for monitoring the range of research topics. This prevents one topic area from becoming saturated and others from being under-researched;
- protection of funding bodies, healthcare organizations and universities from rogue practices and potential litigation;
- acting as a forum for discussion of best practice.

In order to assure the quality of research, local and central ethics committees vet all potential studies that:

- involve NHS patients, relatives or carers;
- involve the study of sensitive topic areas;
- involve using NHS staff;
- involve needing access to data, bodily materials of past or present patients;
- involve using foetal material;
- will involve the use of or access to NHS premises and equipment.

Despite the positive features of ethics committees there are a number of difficulties that require some consideration. The first issue concerns the process of submitting the research proposal. All researchers submit research applications in a uniform manner via an online system called The Integrated Research Application System (IRAS). The forms are comprehensive but are also time-consuming due to the depth of information that is required. Ethics committees tend to meet sporadically which can result in the delayed processing of approvals and rejections. This causes great concern for researchers and can lead to erroneous perceptions of ethics committees as blockers or barriers to research projects. Some researchers and research students perceive ethics committees as 'research police' whose primary role is to reject research projects. However, Parahoo (2006) highlights that mutual benefits exist in that ethics committees have an additional role in guiding researchers in acceptable practices and assisting in developing their potential research skills in addition to protecting the researcher and their organization from potential litigation.

One would assume that the introduction of local and central ethics committees would result in ethically sound studies. However, Crookes and Davies (2004) claim that the approval process is not uniform and different criteria result in some studies being approved in one district while other research studies are rejected in another district. MacDuff et al. (2007) add that ethical committees are the norm in many countries such as European countries, USA, Australia and Canada, but developing countries have yet to establish adequate systems for evaluating the ethical quality of their studies as they have yet to be convinced of their real purpose.

Exercise 8.4

Identify the key elements of an ethical piece of research. Answers are provided in the Appendix.

Research governance

The UK government introduced *The Research Governance Framework for Health and Social Care* in 2001 (Department of Health 2001) with a view to reducing unacceptable variations in research strategies. Research governance is now recognized as a core standard for every healthcare organization that carries out research. The aims of the Framework were to:

- improve the quality of research;
- safeguard the well being of the public;
- promote good research practice and learn lessons from history;
- prevent poor performance and misconduct;
- ensure that the rights and dignity of participants and the general public are protected.

The Research Governance Framework for Health and Social Care set national ethical standards, describes appropriate monitoring and review procedures and defines the mechanisms that are required to deliver the standards that have been set. In addition to these roles the Framework positively encourages and promotes research activity in health care by claiming to 'Provide a context for the encouragement of creative and innovative research and for the effective transfer of learning, technology and best practice to improve care' (Department of Health 2001: 3). Although the Framework encourages innovation and the creation of new knowledge it firmly advocates that this knowledge must have rigorous methods and clearly-defined questions that are relevant for modern society. All decision-making processes must be transparent with clear lines of responsibility and accountability. Researchers must report any adverse events and learn lessons by sharing experiences through learning networks. *The Research Governance Framework for Health and Social Care* became British Law in 2004 and it is every researcher's duty to become familiar with the Framework and to adhere to its principles. There are several rationales for introducing research governance:

- lapses in ethical behaviour: for example, in the Willowbrook study in 1972 (Krugman 1972) mentally-impaired children were only allowed access to a residential treatment facility if their parents consented to their participation in a research study that involved being injected with the hepatitis virus;
- lack of knowledge regarding the ethical principles and processes required for research purposes: for example, Parahoo (2006) highlights that some universities have no formal ethical processes;
- new technologies and research techniques such as cloning and embryonic research.

Exercise 8.5

Read the following article by Fontenla and Rycroft-Malone. This provides a clear overview of research governance and highlights the strengths and weaknesses of the research governance framework.

Fontenla, M. and Rycroft-Malone, J. (2006) Research governance and ethics: a resource for novice researchers, *Nursing Standard*, 20(23): 41–6.

Summary

This chapter has discussed the ethical principles that are used to assure the proper and moral conduct of research studies. Research participants have been identified as vulnerable due to their lack of research knowledge, their position as a captive population or lack of capacity to make informed decisions. Researchers often have to make difficult decisions regarding who to include and who to exclude in a study and the potential risks and benefits to the participants must be evaluated. Four *prima facie* have been identified as crucial to protecting the ethical rights of participants and each of these has been discussed in depth. Respect for autonomy considers the extent to which participants can make informed decisions and in order to assure this capacity to consent must be considered. Doing good, preventing harm and operating in a fair manner have been identified as fundamental ethical principles that are used to protect the basic human rights of research participants. Additional strategies include the Research Governance Framework and the use of ethics committees which jointly set and evaluate the standards that are required to guarantee ethically robust research. Although strategies exist to assure the quality of research studies these should not compensate for the ethical awareness of the researcher. Appropriate skills, good human insight and appropriate moral judgements are the cornerstone to good research.

Reflective activity

Imagine that a researcher approaches you to take part in a clinical trial for a new drug. How would you feel about taking part? What might your concerns be? What behaviours, legislations and attitudes would you want to see in place?

Jargon busting

Make a list of any words in this chapter that you do not understand. Look up their meaning and consider their use in the world of research. You may identify some of the following words and terms:

Anonymity: This concerns the extent to which the participant can be linked to their responses.
Autonomy: Respecting a person's decision-making capacity.
Beneficence: The act of doing good.
Capacity: Having ability to perform a task.
Coercion: Applying pressure or rewards in order to persuade someone to comply.
Confidentiality: Respecting an individual's right to privacy.
Ethics: Moral principles that guide actions.
Ethics committee: A group of people who evaluate research proposals.
Justice: The act of treating people fairly.
Morals: The personal values that guide the way in which a person acts.
Non-maleficence: The act of preventing harm.
Prima facie: A legal term meaning 'on the face of it' used in ethics to refer to four ethical principles.
Veracity: The act of telling the truth.
Vulnerability: Being in a position of risk or when a person can be taken advantage of.
Without prejudice: The act of respecting an individual's right to withdraw from a study without any bad feeling or repercussions.

References

Beauchamp, T.L. and Childress, J.F. (1989) *The Principles of Biomedical Ethics*. Oxford: Oxford University Press.

Burns, N. and Grove, S. (2005) *The Practice of Nursing Research: Conduct, Critique and Utilization.* CA: Sage Thousand Oaks.

Crookes, P.A. and Davies, S. (2004) *Research into Practice: Essential Skills for Reading and Applying Research in Nursing and Health Care.* London: Bailliere Tindall.

Department of Health (2001) *The Research Governance Framework for Health and Social Care.* London: Department of Health.

Department of Health (2005) *The Mental Capacity Act.* London: Department of Health.

Hem, M.H., Heggen, K. and Ruyter, K.W. (2007) Questionable requirement for consent in observational research in psychiatry, *Nursing Ethics*, 14(1): 41–53.

Krugman, S. (1972) The Willowbrook study revisited, *Journal of American Medical Association*, 222: 928–30.

MacDuff, C., McKie, A., Martindale, S. et al. (2007) A novel framework for reflecting on the functioning of research ethics review panels, *Nursing Ethics*, 14(1): 99–115.

Margalith, I., Tabak, N. and Granot, T. (2008) Student nurses' care of terrorists and their victims, *Nursing Ethics*, 15(5): 601–14.

Moule, P. and Goodman, M. (2009) *Nursing Research: An Introduction.* Thousand Oaks, CA: Sage.

Nursing and Midwifery Council (2008) *The Code of Professional Conduct.* London: NMC.

Parahoo, K. (2006) *Nursing Research: Principles, Process and Issues.* New York: Palgrave Macmillan.

Polgar, T. (2008) *Introduction to Research in the Health Sciences.* London: Churchill Livingstone.

Richards, H.M. and Schwarts, L.J. (2002) Ethics of qualitative research: are there special issues for health service research? *Family Practice*, 19(2): 13.

World Medical Association (2008) *The Declaration of Helsinki.* Helsinki, Finland.

Further reading

Bell, J. (2009) *Doing your Research Project: A Guide for First-time Researchers in Education, Health and Social Science*, 4th edn. Maidenhead: Open University Press.

The Social Research Association (SRA) provides some useful guidelines for novice researchers and has established an ethics forum to resolve ethical dilemmas in research and promote ethical reflection. Website: http://www.the-sra.org.uk/ethical.htm

9 Searching for literature

Introduction

In order to comprehend research you will need to compare and contrast the writings of different authors and at some point in your studies you will have to search for information in order to complete assignments. The aim of a literature search is to find good-quality evidence to support your decisions. Conducting a literature search is a very labour-intensive process that involves using paper resources and electronic resources. Using a systematic approach and managing your records effectively will make the process more manageable. The aim of this chapter is to introduce you to the practicalities of literature searching.

Learning outcomes

At the end of this chapter you will be able to:

- rationalize the need for a literature review;
- identify strategies for successful literature searching;
- identify relevant search engines and databases;
- demonstrate an understanding of the terms Boolean operators, truncation and wildcards;
- recognize the potential pitfalls when searching for literature.

Why carry out a literature review?

The notion of reviewing literature is not new. Leach et al. (2009) claim that Bacon (c1214–1294), Copernicus (1473–1543) and Galileo (1564–1642) all reviewed the theories that existed when they developed their knowledge bases in philosophy. In the current evidence based culture it is every healthcare professional's duty to be up to date with contemporary practice. In order to be credible in changing healthcare practices, health workers need to apply a body of evidence rather than trying to make change on the basis of one piece of research. Reviewing all of the available literature around a topic area demonstrates that the healthcare professional has read extensively and has a thorough comprehension of the topic area, adding merit to their credibility as a change agent.

In order to influence practice, research needs to have a strong theoretical base and should be evaluated for its strengths and weaknesses in light of all other available evidence. Reviewing the literature identifies flaws and gaps in knowledge that can be used to justify the feasibility of the topic under investigation and avoids studies being unnecessarily repeated for academic purposes. For academic development, carrying out a literature review can add focus to the research area and can raise further questions that are worthy of investigation. Aveyard (2007) refers to this as moving from the known to the unknown as research conclusions often create more questions than answers. We can see that a literature review has some very fundamental functions in terms of service redesign and development and providing a platform for theoretical growth. A comprehensive literature review is only as good as the researcher's knowledge of search indexes and databases and the amount of focus towards the topic area.

Defining the parameters

The starting point of a good literature search is to ascertain exactly what it is that you want to know. This may involve writing a question that needs to be answered or writing a sentence that encompasses all of the key concepts that you wish to explore. It is often a good idea to create a spider-graph on a blank piece of paper that allows you to brainstorm all of your ideas. This will allow you to clearly identify the topic, the concepts that need to be investigated and the key words that need to be used in your search strategy. It is often useful to start being generic and work to the specific. This task involves being very clear about the topic area and selecting inclusion and exclusion criteria.

Choosing an appropriate topic

If you are searching literature for academic purposes your topic should be discussed with your tutor as you need to choose a topic that has already been written about or you will not have sufficient material to discuss. Sometimes literature searches fail because the topic area is too narrow and not enough papers are identified, and sometimes the literature search identifies so many articles that it would be impossible to access them all. For example, at this moment in time there are 12,700,000 articles about diabetes available to download from Google.

Exercise 9.1

From the following list identify which topics would be suitable to study and which ones would be unsuitable. Answers are provided in the Appendix.

1   The arch of the rainbow as a metaphor for caring.
2   Patients' perceptions of patient controlled analgesia as a method of pain relief.
3   Diabetic care in the USA.
4   Physiotherapists' perceptions of work-related stress in the British NHS.
5   The bio-psycho-social manifestations of playing Robbie Williams music in patients with acute repetitive strain injury.

Inclusion and exclusion criteria

The rationale for setting inclusion and exclusion criteria is to establish focus and relevance; it is easy to get sidetracked due to the large amount of data that is available. In order to limit your search you need to define the parameters in terms of the language used, the time period and the types of journals that you wish to access. This is not a one-off process and may involve constantly reviewing and refining your criteria.

Language

You may wish to only include articles that have been written in the English language and may select this as your inclusion criteria, but this may identify too many articles and may include articles from countries that differ significantly from your own in terms of their healthcare provision. Therefore you may wish to limit the search to articles from European countries or only articles from USA, Canada or Australia, China, Scandinavia, etc. However, be aware that by limiting your search in this way you could exclude some potentially useful work.

You will need to define the key words that are relevant to your topic area and identify any associated key words. It is important to be specific as search engines cannot access your brain; they can only attempt to find appropriate matches for the exact words that you enter. For example, you may wish to explore the subject of acute pain following surgery. To do this

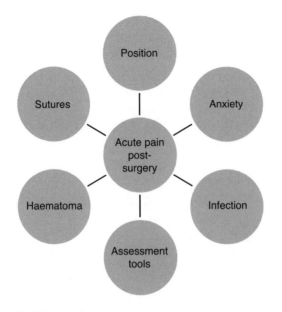

Figure 9.1   Associated key words.

your key words would be: acute, pain, surgery. Your associated words may be: anxiety, positional, assessment tools, infection, haematoma, sutures. You could summarize these visually such as in Figure 9.1.

Key terms and words can be linked or excluded through the use of Boolean operators which are basically just words that connect with others. For example, if you were writing an assignment about the impact of exercise upon diabetes you would use the search words diabetes AND exercise; AND would be an example of a Boolean operator. The database will only identify articles that have diabetes and exercise in their title. Other examples include using words such as IN and OR. If you want to exclude irrelevant material you could use the term NOT as a Boolean operator; for example, you could specify diabetes mellitus NOT gestational diabetes.

Many databases will only search for the exact word that you put in but using truncation can enable you to identify similar words that exist that are nearly the same as the key word. For example, if your key word is care using car$ or * can identify any variations such as caring, carer. Some countries use the same word but with a different spelling and using a wildcard can allow these words to be identified. Wildcards are placed in the centre of a word where a possible variation could occur. For example, if the terms paediatric and pediatric are used an example of a wildcard could be to type in p?ediatric and both spellings would be identified.

Time periods

You will find the most up-to-date literature in journals but may also need to access classic pieces of literature to set the scene or support more current findings. Up-to-date research is research that has been written within the last five years but often older works have relevance and are useful in supporting the need for change. Setting very strict exclusion criteria can result in seminal pieces of work being excluded, which limits the depth and substance of the work.

Types of literature to be accessed

It is good practice to use primary research rather than secondary sources in a literature search as these are reported first hand and are not influenced by anyone else's subjective interpretation. For academic purposes journals are the key resource for most literature searches as this is where the most recent and most innovative work relating to practice will be found. Textbooks can be useful in setting the scene but tend to date very quickly compared to journal articles. Depending on the reason for your literature search you may wish to include or exclude unpublished work and policy documents. Several authors argue that restricting the search to unpublished work can result in a bias that stems from publishers being highly selective in the types of articles that they perceive as relevant. Unpublished work is referred to as 'grey literature' and is often harder to find than published work. Some libraries have a specific section for dissertations and policy documents.

Exercise 9.2

Identify a topic area that you wish to explore either for personal interest, academic purposes or for clinical practice. Write down the inclusion and exclusion criteria for your proposed literature search.

Databases and search engines

Once you have identified your search criteria you can start the practical process of locating literature. Literature can be accessed in hard copy through libraries or online through the internet. Most academic and NHS libraries stock the most popular national and international journals in their periodicals section. Most libraries have an electronic cataloguing system which contains details of all of the available literature; this can save you valuable time and means that you do not have to randomly search the shelves. Searches can be performed by using specific authors, key words or subject matter. You may find Copac a very useful resource as this is a comprehensive catalogue of the largest libraries within the UK and Ireland. The Joanna Briggs Institute in Australia is a useful source for finding summaries of best practice for nurses and can be accessed at http://www.joannabriggs.edu.au/pubs/best_practice.php and the Cochrane Library is the best place to identify systematic reviews. For behavioural and social science students the Campbell Collaboration provides systematic reviews concerning the outcomes of interventions and can be accessed at http://www.campbellcollaboration.org/fralibrary.html.

It is important to note that electronic searching is not one hundred per cent accurate and may fail to identify every relevant article. This may be due to the key words that the authors have used in their titles as some titles do not accurately reflect the nature of the work. For example, below are some titles of articles that could be confusing for readers and may not be included in a primary literature search about caring:

- *Have we Arrived or are we on the Way Out? Promises, Possibilities and Paradigms*
- *Robb, Dock and Nutting: I Wish I'd Been There.*
- *Caritas and Communitas: An Ethic for Caring Science.*

These examples demonstrate that rather than relying on titles alone, it is sometimes wise to access the abstract for each identified article in order to ascertain its usefulness. There is no single strategy that will enable you to identify all of the available information that you require and you will often find additional data by reviewing the references provided at the end of the articles that you have retrieved. This is rather like a snowballing effect where accessing data leads to accessing more and more data. Multiple approaches will yield the most useful data and include hand-searching indexes and scrutinizing the publications from recent conferences. Indexes are the hard copy equivalents of electronic databases. The number of journals available has made the use of indexes almost redundant as electronic searching is quicker, a wider selection of journals can be accessed and the databases can be updated more easily. Unfortunately most databases are produced by commercial companies and require subscriptions. As a student or a health professional you will have free access to some databases. Below is a list of useful databases for healthcare research:

- AMED (Allied and Complementary Medicine Database) produced by the British Library: this database is particularly useful for medicine, nurses, physiotherapists, occupational therapists, complementary medicine and palliative care.

- ASSIA (Applied Social Sciences Index and Abstracts): this database is useful for healthcare professionals working in the social sciences and health visiting.
- Australasian Medical Index: this database is useful for medicine and allied healthcare professionals but not all of the work is transferable into healthcare systems that differ from the Australian healthcare system.
- British Nursing Index: a nursing and midwifery database.
- CANCERLIT: a database for information about cancer.
- Centre for Reviews and Dissemination (http://www.york.ac/inst/crd): this centre reviews all of the available work around health care and provides comprehensive systematic reviews.
- CINAHL (Cumulative Index to Nursing and Allied Health Literature): this database is useful for nurses and allied healthcare professionals.
- Embase: this database is very useful for pharmacists and prescribing students.
- ERIC: this is an education-based database.
- IBBS (International Bibliography of the Social Sciences): this database is useful for social workers, health visitors and allied healthcare professionals.
- International Nursing Index: this database is useful for nurses.
- MEDLINE: this database is very useful for medicine and allied healthcare professionals and is particularly useful for accessing randomized control trials.
- PsychLit: this database is useful for those employed in the mental health sphere.
- System for Information on Grey Literature in Europe: this database will highlight any grey literature relevant to your topic.

Many students ask the question 'when do I stop searching?' There is no right answer to this question; it is a very personal and pragmatic decision. Often you will reach a point when the same articles keep reappearing over and over again and no new material becomes available. This is an appropriate time to cease the search but additional factors such as the time and resources available will also impact the decision.

Exercise 9.3

Using truncation and wildcards, select an appropriate database and perform a search for your identified keywords. Keep a record of any problems that you encounter.

Record keeping

It is very important to document your search strategy as this provides the evidence for your systematic approach. Stringent records of the search terms and results are useful references to draw upon when additional data is required or if you accidentally get distracted by interesting but irrelevant articles. Record keeping enables you to track where combined searches have been performed and identify which searches provided the most useful results. If you are exploring a topic that is very relevant to your role and the topic is one that you may continue to explore in more depth your search strategy will save you very valuable time in the future. It is also useful to document any articles that you were unable to retrieve as these may become available online at a later date. Articles can be stored by adding each one as a favourite on your home PC and can be saved as bookmarks in del.icio.us. The advantage of using del.icio.us is that articles can be shared with colleagues and a network of like-minded individuals can be developed.

Accessing the data

Accessing the data need not occur at the end of the literature search; it is more prudent to access literature as you identify it as this will allow you the time and opportunity to identify further data through snowballing. Many students make the mistake of printing and photocopying every article that they find which is expensive and can result in excessive and irrelevant data. It is wiser to print out the abstracts and review these thoroughly in order to appraise the usefulness of individual articles. At this stage it is useful to refer back to your inclusion and exclusion criteria in order to focus your search. It is easy to get lost in the literature and lose direction or become diverted by romantic notions that may be interesting but not relevant. One of the most useful resources to your search will be your local librarian who can be a crucial link to obtaining the data that you require. You do not need to search alone; the best literature searches involve using every available resource.

Exercise 9.4

Access and read the following user-friendly articles about literature searching aimed at novice researchers and students:

> Hendry, C. and Farley, A. (1998) Reviewing the literature: a guide for students, *Nursing Standard*, 12(44): 46–48.
> Younger, P. (2004) Using the internet to conduct a literature search, *Nursing Standard*, 19(6): 45–51.

Summary

This chapter has discussed the importance of adopting a systematic approach when searching for literature. Four key stages have been identified as:

- define the parameters of the search;
- identify the search strategy;
- record the search strategy;
- access the data.

Each of these four stages have been discussed as discrete elements when in reality they actually occur in a cyclical fashion with refinement occurring at any stage in the cycle. The literature search cycle can be summarized as in Figure 9.2. This demonstrates that literature searching is not performed as a single activity but requires constant review and adjustment. Students always ask the question: 'How many articles do I need?' The only answer can be that it is quality and not quantity that matters. Twenty relevant articles are better than fifty partially relevant ones. It is how the data is used that matters not the number of references that appear at the end of a dissertation. It is a sad fact that literature searches are often performed as part of an academic assessment and not often used to develop new ideas as a practical norm. This results in searching being stressful and often rushed when it could be performed at a leisurely pace as issues of interest arise in practice. The next chapter will discuss how to critically review the data once it has been accessed but it is

Figure 9.2 The cycle of literature searching.

important to remember that the quality of the findings is only as good as the quality of the literature search.

Reflective activity

Consider the pros and cons of carrying out a literature review. What skills do you think that you could gain from this activity?

Jargon busting

Make a list of any words in this chapter that you do not understand. Look up their meaning and consider their use in the world of research. You may identify some of the following words and terms:

Boolean operators: Words that can be used to limit the parameters of a search.
Exclusion criteria: The material that you wish to exclude from your literature search.
Inclusion criteria: The material that you consider to be vital to your search topic.
Truncation symbols: Symbols that can be inserted into words that identify similar words or phrases.

References

Aveyard, H. (2007) *Doing a Literature Review in Health and Social Care: A Practical Guide*. Maidenhead: Open University Press.
Leach, M., Neale, J., Kemp, P.A. (2009) Literature reviews, in: J. Neale (ed.) *Research Methods for Health and Social Care*. Basingstoke: Palgrave Macmillan.

Further reading

For information on how to carry out a literature review, access the above references and the following:

Hart, C. (1998) *Doing a Literature Review: Releasing the Social Science Research Imagination*. London: Sage.
Hart, C. (2001) *Doing a Literature Search: A Comprehensive Guide for Social Sciences*. London: Sage.

Hek, G. and Moule, P. (2006) *Making Sense of Research: An Introduction for Health and Social Care Practitioners*. London: Sage.

Watkinson, N. (2008) Literature searching and using the internet efficiently and effectively, in: M. Lloyd and P. Murphy (eds) *Essential Study Skills for Health and Social Care*. Exeter: Reflective Press.

10 Critically reviewing literature

Introduction

Thinking begins at birth and is practised almost instinctively throughout life, so one would assume that transferring this skill into evidence based practice would be effortless. Yet critical thinking appears to be a great source of anxiety for the majority of research students. Despite the assumption that we engage in critical thought subconsciously, van Gelder (2004) argues that humans are not natural critical thinkers. He stresses that humans are, by their nature, pattern-seeking, story-telling animals who prefer to maintain the status quo rather than to challenge existing patterns of practice. In order to apply evidence in a meaningful way that is relevant to practice, health professionals need to open their minds to the options available to them; this means challenging convention and supporting their convictions through the critical application of research based evidence. The aim of this chapter is to liberate the student from ritualistic practice and increase their confidence to challenge the findings from literature.

Learning outcomes

At the end of this chapter you will be able to:

- consider the rationales for critical thinking;
- demonstrate comprehension of the process of critical thinking;
- approach literature in a more questioning manner;
- apply the technique of critical thinking to practice.

Why should we think critically?

Healthcare professionals have a moral mandate to be critical thinkers as health care is concerned with the care of vulnerable people. Health service users deserve the best care available. You can only give the best if you know what the best is and you can only know what the best is by investigating the options available. In order to make an informed clinical decision you need to develop well-founded arguments and present reliable and valid evidence. Computer aided resources such as the internet have resulted in more assertive and knowledgeable patients and clients who demand to be involved in selecting from the range of services that exist. However, these people remain vulnerable to both the safe and reliable data and the dross that appears on un-reviewed websites. The lay public may not be healthy enough to logically appraise the literature that impacts their care so they may need protection and advocacy. Poorly-informed health professionals cannot offer the level of advocacy and security that patients deserve as they lack the skills required to recognize the charlatans. Thinking critically allows you to differentiate the significant from the insignificant and separate the fact from the fiction.

It is important to remember that health professionals are people and, as such, do not exist in a healthcare 'bubble'. Critical thinking is a lifelong transferable skill that gives you the confidence to challenge long-held assumptions in a constructive and confident manner outside of the healthcare arena. Consciously appraising options and choices increases personal confidence in decision making and strengthens one's own personal character.

What is critical thinking?

Critical thinking is a process of deliberation (Cottrell 2005). This implies that it is learned and ordered. To be actualized to its full potential it requires the ability to scrutinize, rationalize and prioritize. Many people mistakenly equate critiquing with criticizing. Criticism carries negative connotations and is usually an opportunity to express negative and biased opinions or views without consciously appraising the true value of the subject. In contrast, critiquing is concerned with objectively evaluating the worth of a piece of literature. While criticism is concerned with closing the mind to opportunities, critiquing is concerned with liberating the thinking process and opening the mind. 'Critical thinking is the starting point of dialogue whereas criticism is the end of the conversation' (Ross 2008: 218).

Van Gelder (2004) refers to critical thinking as a higher order skill implying that it occurs cumulatively once lower order skills have been internalized. For example, if you consider the activity of gymnastics, most humans have the capacity to perform some elements of gymnastics but we are not born with these skills. First we have to learn to walk, then we have to learn to run, then learn how to balance and tumble; these lower order skills have to be mastered before we can expect to be able to perform back-flips. The same principles can be applied to the process of critical thinking in that you need to read literature then comprehend the content, identify logic, analyse findings, synthesize multiple data and then theorize. Like any form of activity, it needs practice in order to become a skill. This could be likened to becoming fluent in a second language. Critical thinking is a six stage process concerned with:

- critically reading the literature;
- identifying the premise within the literature;
- being sceptical by evaluating the logic;
- appraising the strength of the evidence;
- integrating the logic and evidence to form a balanced viewpoint;
- reflecting upon the potential impact of the conclusions.

Critically reading the literature

You cannot be a critical thinker and writer if you are not a critical reader. Close and copious reading is essential as one cannot be critical in the absence of options from which to draw upon. Students often ask the questions 'how many references do I need and how much do I need to read?' The answers are 'as many as are relevant' and 'more than you think'. The more text that you engage with, the greater your understanding will be. However, in order to engage with text, you need to focus and interact with the messages within it, and you can only achieve this if the text is set at the correct level. Many students make the mistake of accessing higher level texts that they fail to interact with, when it is better to start with literature that feels comfortable and build on this as your confidence grows. Close reading requires commitment, time and concentration. Close reading is not just absently looking at words; it involves questioning the literature and examining the meaning within it. Critical reading involves moving from the general to the specific by skim reading first and then focusing intently on the messages within the text to understand its significance.

Identifying the premise within the literature

Every author is selling you a viewpoint. They seek to convert you; to manipulate your beliefs and attitudes through a covert messaging system. They start by selling you a premise or a proposition that they wish you to consider and support this by adding contributing arguments and evidence. This can be translated as the *message* which is communicated, encoded and decoded in order to understand it. The message is usually threaded throughout the text but can also be explicitly stated as a problem statement or hypothesis. Although this sounds calculating, it is true of every piece of work. We all have viewpoints and without a starting point, the text would have no opportunity to progress. The starting point for analysing the text is to ask the question 'what is this author telling me, and what is the premise that he/she is trying to sell?' You should read a whole piece of text and identify the premise within the whole and then analyse each paragraph individually to identify if any other premises exist.

Exercise 10.1

Identify the premise in the following fictitious piece of text:

In the last few years, the use of narratives has become more noticeable in health-care literature. People are at last recognizing the value of story telling. Smith (2010) claims that there were over thirty-five articles published in the *Journal of Effective Healthcare* that used the narrative approach this year. This demonstrates that narratives are gaining credibility as a research method in health care. Clyde (2009) carried out a meta-analysis of narrative research studies carried out between 2000 and 2008 and noticed a dramatic increase in the number of researchers using this method. Jones (2005) claims that narrative research is the best method of identifying the patient's real experience of health care.

Exercise 10.2

Which of these is the author's premise?

1   Most researchers like using the narrative method to gain data about health care.
2   Patients value the narrative method more than other methods.
3   The narrative method is becoming more popular.
4   Narratives are gaining credibility as a research method in health care.
5   Narratives are not very popular.

Answer: The answer is provided below to enhance your understanding.

In this example numbers 3 and 4 are the most likely choices; however, only one of them is the actual premise. The author is selling you the message that the narrative method is gaining credibility as a research method and supports this with all of the additional narrative. For this reason, 4 is the correct answer. Although the text highlights that narratives are becoming more popular and provides evidence to support this from Clyde (2009) these sentences support the notion that the popularity is linked to credibility. Identifying the author's premise can sometimes be difficult as very similar points may be present; you need to identify the key points and pay close attention to detail. Cottrell (2005) claims that capturing the author's premise involves identifying two types of arguments:

- the overall argument which is the author's position about an issue;
- contributing arguments which are the additional bits of information in support of the overall argument.

Exercise 10.3

Can you identify any contributing arguments in the text in Exercise 10.1? Answers are provided in the Appendix.

Being sceptical by evaluating the logic

Being sceptical involves opening the mind to different ways of thinking. Cottrell (2005) refers to scepticism as holding polite doubt and questioning what you read. Scepticism is not about doubting everything that you read; people need to have some trust in the world in order to exist within it. Needleman (2004) says be open-minded but not so open-minded that your brains fall out. Too much scepticism results in a failure to commit to anything and too little leads to gullibility. There are two distinct phases to evaluating the literature: stage one involves analysing the logic in the text and stage two involves analysing the robustness of the evidence. Once you have identified the logic it is easier to identify the key issues and assumptions that need to be explored and challenged and to evaluate whether the author's premise needs more support. Analysing the logic in the text involves questioning the extent to which the author's premise is trustworthy or believable. First, you need to evaluate the extent to which the author's claims fit with reality as you know it.

In order to do this you need to ask the following questions:

- What is the author's premise?
- Do I believe it?
- What rationales exist in the world to lead me to believe it?
- Who else agrees with this view?
- Is there any additional support for the viewpoint?
- Why should I not believe it?
- How does the author's premise not fit with my world view?
- Is there any evidence to negate the viewpoint?

Basically, as the reader, you are looking for rationality in the claims. Achieving this task involves being sceptical by seeking out the various viewpoints that exist within additional literature and identifying arguments for and against the author's premise. The reader must compare and contrast the multiple views that exist in order to accept or reject the author's viewpoint. It is important to note that this process is not about seeking truth in the literature; it is about searching for evidence. There are no right or wrong answers as different students may have different world views; it is being able to support these views that matters.

If we return to the text in Exercise 10.1, we can apply the principles of sceptical thought and identify any support or refutation for the author's premise.

You need to ask yourself, do you believe that narratives are gaining credibility as a research method in health care? In order to answer this you need to investigate what you know about narrative research: do narratives have any relevance to health care? Can narrative research address healthcare concerns? How can it achieve this? Is there any support for this view within this piece of text? Is there any support for this view in other pieces of literature? Is there an obvious increase in the use of narratives within healthcare journals in general? Is there any evidence within the literature that does not support the view that narratives are gaining credibility? The reader needs to evaluate the strength of the logic in each author's work, put the arguments together and come to a conclusion regarding the sensibility of the premise. The second stage involves evaluating the strength of the evidence implicit within the premise.

Appraising the strength of the literature

The extent to which an author's viewpoint can be believed is dependent upon the extent to which the author can provide adequate support for the premise. Van Gelder (2004) argues that we often seek out evidence that supports our beliefs and avoid literature that contradicts them. We tend to rate evidence as good or bad depending upon whether it supports our viewpoint. Confusion exists about what constitutes good evidence and exactly what counts as evidence. If we return to the text in Exercise 10.1, we can see that the author provides several forms of evidence in support of the premise.

First the author states that the use of narratives has become more noticeable in the literature and that people are recognizing the value of story telling. However, the author fails to provide any additional support for these statements; they are the author's viewpoint and are referred to as *anecdotal evidence*. The author provides three additional types of evidence to support the premise in the form of: a meta-analysis of all of the research articles over an eight year period (Clyde 2009), case evidence from one type of healthcare journal in a one-year period (Smith 2010) and an anecdotal point of view from one author (Jones 2005).

Several authors (McClarey and Duff 1997; Moule and Goodman 2009) suggest that evidence can be evaluated according to a hierarchy such as that provided by McClarey and Duff (1997).

1   a meta-analysis of all randomized control trials concerning a partic-ular topic;
2   one robust randomized control trial;
3   evidence from a non-randomized control trial;
4   a robust survey;
5   a good, well-planned qualitative study;
6   a literature review that examines all of the work available on a topic;
7   the work of an expert;
8   multiple opinions about a topic area from people who are not experts;
9   one opinion-based, anecdotal piece of work.

Exercise 10.4

Using McClarey and Duff's hierarchy, can you identify where levels of evidence exist for the text used in the practice example in Exercise 10.4? How strong is the evidence used to support the premise?

It is argued that hierarchies of evidence promote positivism as having superiority and neglect to recognize the value of qualitative evidence. It could be argued that rigid hierarchies also overlook the importance of personal knowledge in the decision-making process.

Many students ask the question 'How do I know what to look for when critiquing a study?' The answer I give is 'you need to decide if a study is sub-stantive enough to support the premise and are the methodological decisions appropriate for the question and the intention of the research?' You need to unpack the research and pull it apart in order to analyse its components. You can only do this if you have a good understanding of research as without this you cannot identify the strengths and weaknesses. All studies contain flaws but if every study with a flaw was discarded there would be no studies left to critique. Just as every study has flaws, it also has strengths. Recognizing the strengths and weaknesses broadens understanding and helps to build a solid foundation for research knowledge. Furthermore, recognizing flaws pre-vents further flaws occurring which results in more robust research in the future.

Several models exist to help students evaluate the rigour of research studies such as Cormack (2006), Cottrell (2005), Polgar and Thomas (2008) and Burns and Grove (2005). Most of these guides provide a set of generic questions and differ greatly in their content. However, the general rule is to follow the structure of the research article as most articles are similar in the processes that they follow. All research should be evaluated in terms of structure, methods, ethics, theoretical consistency, reliability and validity. We will now examine each of these in turn:

Structure

- The starting point for critiquing an article needs to address how current the article is as this will impact its relevance for practice. Articles that are more than five years old may have limited clinical relevance and their ability to change practice is greatly reduced the older they are.
- Second, any potential biases that stem from the researchers position should be identified. For example, has the research been sponsored by a pharmaceutical company with a particular interest in the research topic? Does the author have a particular viewpoint that could impact the direction of the research?
- The research question and title of the work should be critically questioned for their relevance to the study content. The title should accurately reflect the substance of the article and not be constrained by ambiguous language and jargon that can mislead the reader.
- Every article should have an abstract that concisely summarizes the research strategy, methods, findings and implications for practice. The abstract determines the relevancy of the article for the reader and should be an accurate reflection of the research article.
- The philosophical underpinnings of the research should be clearly identified and consistent with the research strategy. For example, if the purpose of the study is to explore perceptions an experimental approach would be inconsistent with the theories of interpretivism.
- The research aims and objectives and hypotheses should be clearly stated and achievable by the research strategy. Often students have to search for this data and sometimes construct their own interpretations which can distort their understanding of the findings.
- The literature review if required should demonstrate sufficient understanding of the current theories and evidence in order to reflect the current state of knowledge. Key policy documents, classic literature and current studies should be included in an unbiased way and their relevance to practice should be established.

- There should be clearly defined methods, ethics and findings sections, and a comprehensive discussion section that identifies the research's relevance for practice. The article should conclude by highlighting any limitations and potential biases.

Methods

A well-constructed methods section is crucial to understanding the nature of the research article. Various authors provide comprehensive frameworks to guide readers on how to review qualitative and quantitative studies as the nature of the study will determine the types of questions that need to be asked. For extensive guidance see Parahoo (2006) and Burns and Grove (2005). However, there are some issues that should always be addressed:

- The sampling method should be explicitly stated and rationalized. It is not unusual for writers to omit their sampling rationales and details of their sampling strategy. Authors should state who they sampled, from which population they were acquired, how many people were sampled, the response rates, and how they dealt with any potential or actual problems such as low response rates or lack of representativeness or reduced homogeneity. Authors should explain exactly how they accessed their samples and ensure that all ethical codes were adhered to. For example, it must be clear that participants were not coerced into participating in the research.
- The instruments and data collection techniques should be rationalized within the context of the philosophical underpinnings in order to establish their appropriateness. The design should match the purpose and potential outcomes of the study and the instruments should have evidence of piloting or previous reliability and validity. All variables should be identified including: independent, dependent, demographic, extraneous and confounding variables.
- The analysis of data should be comprehensively discussed and justified. If the author is using a qualitative research strategy one would expect to see evidence of content analysis, thematic analysis, discourse analysis or constant comparative. If a quantitative approach is taken the author should justify whether descriptive or inferential statistics were used or both. The statistical tests applied should be evident and rationalized. It is not sufficiently robust enough for an author to state that SPSS was used as this does not demonstrate the author's competency in the use of statistics.
- The findings should be easy to interpret and should be linked back to any hypotheses and questions stated at the start of the study in order to establish the relevance of the findings. The findings should be

compared with the findings of other studies and linked to potential improvements in practice.

Ethical considerations

A research article is judged to be ethically robust if the author describes how they have complied with ethical codes and practices. For example, details of ethical approval from all relevant agencies must be included. Students performing research as part of their studies must, as a minimum, provide evidence of ethical clearance from their university. Researchers using patients or vulnerable people must have additional approval from their NHS ethics committee and stricter criteria exists for those who wish to use human tissue. There are central issues that should always be evident in any piece of research such as: risks and benefits, moral intentions, informed consent, confidentiality, anonymity, protecting rights and dignity and minimizing harm and discomfort.

Theoretical consistency

The findings of the study should be evaluated in terms of their relevance to theory and practice. If the purpose of the research was to explore perceptions, the views of the participants must make up the majority of the findings. The arguments constructed must be logically consistent and devoid of any contradictory comments and inferences. The reader should be able to follow the steps that have led to the conclusions without any erroneous assumptions being identified. Cottrell (2005) claims that identifying the author's theoretical position in the conclusions of the study helps to identify gaps in the reasoning and any unstated assumptions.

Validity and reliability

All research needs to be judged in order to establish integrity and rigour. In the literature it appears that researchers do not agree about what constitutes good-quality research and different models exist to judge the trustworthiness of work. Quantitative work seems to be judged according to:

- reliability: this concerns the extent to which an instrument consistently measures the construct that it claims to measure;
- generalizability: this is the extent to which the findings of a study can be transferred from one context to another or from one population to another;

- objectivity: this concerns the extent to which researcher bias has been eliminated or controlled for.

Qualitative work is judged according to:

- dependability: this concerns the extent to which a study can be considered consistent in its approach. The reader should be able to follow the path that led to the conclusions;
- credibility: this refers to internal validity and assumes that different groups will have similar understandings of the concept under investigation;
- transferability: this is very similar to the concept of generalizability and is less important in qualitative research than it is in quantitative research. However, some researchers argue that the theory developed should be applicable to some additional audiences and should have relevance to real practice issues;
- confirmability: this refers to the extent to which the researcher's journey can be audited in order to identify processes and procedures.

Validity

Validity is concerned with the extent to which truthfulness can be achieved; for example, the extent to which an instrument measures what it claims to measure. If a researcher is claiming to explore perceptions of caring using semi-structured interviews, the questions asked must reflect general understandings of caring. In other words the interviews must represent the concept in an authentic way. If you imagine going to McDonald's and asking for a beefburger, you would expect to get a round, brown piece of meat that tastes beefy inside a round bread roll; anything else would not be a truthful representation of a McDonald's beefburger. The participant's response is not open to scrutiny as their reality cannot be questioned; it is their personal view of reality and it is therefore truthful to them. Researchers are not seeking to claim that any participant's views are any more or less worthy, they are merely clarifying that the researcher's interpretation of the data accurately reflects the participant's reality. If we return to the example of the beefburger, we are not claiming that a McDonald's burger is any better than a Burger King burger; we are merely claiming that the burger in front of us is a McDonald's beefburger. Holloway and Wheeler (2002) refer to this process as *internal validity* or *face validity* as it concerns the extent to which the findings of the study accurately reflect the aims and objectives and the social reality of the topic.

Holloway and Wheeler add that the most effective way to ensure internal validity is by member checking, where the data is referred back to the participants for clarification such as in the study by Forhan et al. (2010) who explored people's experiences of obesity. Semi-structured interviews were used to investigate the extent to which obese people felt that their obesity impacted their daily occupations. Transcripts from 14 interviews were mailed to the participants for their views; only five participants returned their comments and these confirmed the interpretations of the researcher. Internal validity can also be achieved through *expert validation* where the tools and findings can be referred to a panel of experts in the topic area. However, difficulties arise when trying to define the term expert and to establish exactly how many experts are required. Chavez-Hernandez et al. (2009) used the views of multiple experts when they compared suicide rates between USA and Mexico and found a concordance rate of 86 per cent between judges.

A second type of validity is criterion-related validity which refers to the extent to which the instrument used compares with other similar instruments. For example, if we devised a questionnaire with specific criteria that allowed us to identify a McDonald's beefburger from any other burgers and found that the questionnaire identified every burger as a McDonald's one, we could say that the questionnaire did not have high criterion-related validity as it was not specific enough for the task. If we devised a second questionnaire that included more detailed criteria that detected the McDonald's burger when it was placed with other burgers we could establish a higher level of criterion-related validity. If other similar questionnaires existed that measured types of burgers and our second questionnaire matched these in terms of the results, we could claim to have high criterion-related validity.

Reliability

The less variation an instrument produces each time it is used, the higher its reliability. Reliability is concerned with the extent to which an instrument has repeatability and consistency. There are three levels of reliability:

- *Stability* This measures the extent to which a tool continuously produces the same result each time that it is used. For example, if a person stands on a set of scales five times per day and obtains the same reading, the scales may be perceived as stable. Alternatively, a rowing team claim to be the best rowing team in the UK and in every race that they perform in, they achieve the fastest time until one occasion where one rower drops an oar into the water resulting in a much slower time and an achievement of fourth place. Can the team still claim to be the best rowing team in the UK?
- *Equivalence* This is used to test the strength of the relationship between results obtained by two different researchers. This method is usually used in observational studies where two observers are measuring the same phenomenon and the term *inter-rater reliability* is often

used. Odd et al. (2004) used inter-rater reliability when they investigated whether the introduction of a contrast medium improved the positioning of central venous lines in neonates. Two researchers compared 212 radiographs and their individual conclusions were compared statistically using a co-efficient.

- *Internal consistency* This is concerned with the extent to which all of the subparts of an instrument measure the main construct. If we refer back to the beefburger example and wanted to be sure that the item in front of us was a true McDonald's beefburger, we would investigate all of the components of a McDonald's beefburger and match these criteria with the burger in front of us. A test called Cronbach's alpha would be applied to measure the internal reality of the burger against the criteria. When evaluating text the reader establishes internal consistency if all of the lines of reasoning contribute to the conclusion without inconsistencies or erroneous assumptions. For example:

> Rabbits have big teeth and like to eat carrots, my Uncle John has big teeth and likes carrots, and therefore, my Uncle John is a rabbit. Here, there is insufficient information about rabbits to confirm the assumption. If we add more details about rabbits such as they live in underground warrens, hop, have long ears and furry tails, we can clearly conclude that my Uncle John is not a rabbit.

Despite the variability in techniques and procedures available, most researchers agree that every study should be critiqued for its rigour. For qualitative researchers achieving validity has higher importance than achieving reliability whereas for quantitative researchers achieving reliability is more important than validity. Differences also exist within paradigms as different philosophical stances accept and reject different criteria for rigour. For example, Heideggarian researchers accept the researcher as an instrument and are not concerned with objectivity as a criterion whereas Husserl followers will evaluate a phenomenological study in terms of the degree of objectivity achieved. Variations are acceptable as long as the research's journey is visible; this means that the researcher should present data clearly and give sufficient detail of the study in order to determine its relevance.

Exercise 10.5

Consider how you evaluate phenomena in everyday life. What type of criteria do you use? How effectively could your evaluations be compared with those of other people? How reliable and valid are your criteria?

Integrating the logic and evidence to form a balanced viewpoint

This stage involves comparing and contrasting the variety of works available, forming balanced arguments to support or refute the viewpoints and integrating the findings to formulate sensible conclusions. One piece of evidence may have much strength and may add great support to the premise but one piece of evidence is not enough to make a valid and reliable claim. Evidence may be very convincing in one piece of text and less so in another. One of the biggest challenges to students is integrating the findings from different studies. The theory is that if you can critique one article you can critique multiple articles; the reality is far more complex.

Ross (2008) refers to the process of integration as looking for order in chaos and highlights that readers can commit two major sins during this process. The first sin she refers to as 'sunny day syndrome' where readers deliberately select only that literature which supports the premise and reject any literature that does not support their viewpoint. The second sin is referred to 'focusing on the rain and forgetting the rainbow' where the reader acknowledges all of the available evidence but discredits any pieces that are not congruent with the reader's perspective by highlighting the weaknesses and ignoring the strengths. This results in a biased evaluation of the evidence and produces flawed reasoning.

Integrating the findings involves identifying the strengths and weaknesses in each piece of work and arguing the extent to which authors agree and disagree. Commonalities and differences should be identified and questioned; it is important to establish why viewpoints differ rather than to just identify their existence. Integration involves looking for relationships that exist, assumptions that could be made and explanations that could be used to either formulate theory or form the catalyst for further studies.

Reflecting upon the potential impact of the conclusions

This stage involves pulling all of the information together to form some logical conclusions. The reader evaluates these conclusions in terms of their relevance to practice or the extent to which the conclusions add to a body of knowledge. Sometimes research just confirms what the reader already knows; the importance of this should not be overlooked as confirming good practice and rational thought is a very valuable activity. Change is not a necessary outcome of research. Stretching the mind and critically debating findings is exercise for the brain. Motivation creates more motivation; just as the gymnast becomes more flexible and agile with practice, the brain becomes more alert and more receptive to the wider world. Ross (2008) claims that critical thinking is a craft and like most crafts it needs engagement, commitment and practice.

Summary

This chapter has discussed the process of critical thinking. Critical thinking has been defined as an objective way of analysing literature. Van Gelder (2004) has stressed that critical thinking is a higher order skill that has to be learned and practised; it is not a skill that people are born with. However, it has been described as the key to increasing personal and professional confidence. One cannot make change without critically reviewing the evidence first and healthcare professionals cannot claim to be making evidence based decisions if they have not adequately critiqued the evidence that is available. Critical thinking has been identified as a six-stage process that involves critically reading all of the available literature about a topic, questioning the rationality within the literature, appraising the strength of the evidence and comparing and contrasting the various findings. The conclusions are then drawn together and integrated to form some theory that can be transferred into practice. This chapter has argued that critical thinking is the key to awakening the brain to the potential that exists in the wider world.

Reflective activity

Consider the model that has been discussed throughout this chapter. What do you think are the strengths and weaknesses of using this approach?

Jargon busting

Make a list of any words in this chapter that you do not understand. Look up their meaning and consider their use in the world of research. You may identify some of the following words and terms:

Abstract: A brief summary of the research undertaken.
Anecdotal: Someone's expressed opinion.
Bias: Where the author's personal viewpoint influences the research in some way.
Critical thinking: The process of pulling literature apart and analysing the authors rationality and the strength of the evidence.
Decoding: Interpreting a message that has been sent.
Encoding: Sending a message to a person in a particular language.
Ethics: Codes, principles and beliefs that determine the acceptability of a study.
Hypothesis: A testable statement.
Meta-analysis: An examination of all of the studies that exist about a particular topic. The results are analysed statistically.

Narrative: A research method that analyses stories.
Premise: The message within the text that the author wants you to believe.
Randomized control trial: An experiment that uses randomized sampling.
Reliability: The extent to which a study can be replicated and achieve similar results.
Scepticism: Opening one's mind and questioning.
Validity: The extent to which truthfulness is achieved.

References

Burns, N. and Grove, S.K. (2005) *The Practice of Nursing Research: Conduct, Critique and Utilization*. St Louis, MO: Elsevier Saunders.

Chavez-Hernandez, A.M., Leenaars, A., Chavez-de Sanchez, M.I. and Leenaars, L. (2009) Suicides notes from Mexico and the United States: a thematic analysis, *Salud Publica Mexico*, 51(4): 314–20.

Cormack, D. (2006) *The Research Process in Nursing*. Oxford: Blackwell.

Cottrell, S. (2005) *Critical Thinking Skills: Developing Effective Analysis and Argument*. New York: Palgrave Macmillan.

Forhan, M.A., Law, M.C., Vrkljan, B.H. and Taylor, V.H. (2010) The experience of participation in everyday occupations for adults with obesity, *Canadian Journal of Occupational Therapy*, 77(4): 210–18.

Holloway, I. and Wheeler, S. (2002) *Qualitative Research in Nursing*. Oxford: Blackwell.

McClarey, M. and Duff, L. (1997) Clinical effectiveness and evidence based practice, *Nursing Standard*, 11(51): 1–35.

Moules, P. and Goodman, M. (2009) *Nursing Research: An Introduction*. London: Sage publications.

Needlemen, J. (2004) Book chapter in: Carroll, R.T. (2004) *Becoming a Critical Thinker: A Guide for the New Millenium*. New Jersey: Pearson Custom Publishing.

Odd, D., Page, B., Battin, M. and Harding, J. (2004) Does radio-opaque contrast improve radiographic localisation of percutaneous central venous lines? *British Medical Journal*, 89(1): 41–3.

Parahoo, K. (2006) *Nursing Research: Principles, Process and Issues*. Basingstoke: Palgrave Macmillan.

Polgar, S. and Thomas, S.A. (2008) *Introduction to Research in the Health Sciences*. London: Churchill Livingstone.

Ross, T. (2008) *Critical thinking: a six stage process*, in P. Murphy and M. Lloyd (eds) *Essential Study Skills for Health and Social Care*. Exeter: Reflect Press.

van Gelder, T. (2004) Teaching critical thinking: lessons from cognitive science, *College Teaching*, 45: 1–6.

Appendix
Answers to the exercises

Chapter 1

Exercise 1.2: components of evidence based decision making

- patient choice
- up-to-date research
- clinical expertise
- ethical, legal and professional boundaries
- the resources that are available

Exercise 1.4: factors that would deter you from implementing evidence in your working area

- valuing research
- personal/colleagues'/organization's unwillingness to change
- understanding research terms
- lack skills in critiquing evidence
- lack of time and library resources
- no perceived benefit to the patient
- too much conflicting research

Chapter 2

Exercise 2.3: the differences between a literature review and a systematic review

Literature review	Systematic review
Has one reviewer	Has at least two reviewers or more
Less focused question – often has a topic area as its focus	Very focused research question
Undefined methods of searching and critiquing	Explicit and very rigorous search strategy
No protocol to direct the process	Uses a strict protocol

May have some inclusion and exclusion criteria	Uses very strict inclusion and exclusion criteria
Results are presented as a narrative	Findings are often analysed using a meta-analysis with statistics
Low reliability and the results are not easily repeatable by other researchers	High reliablity, results are easily repeatable
Limited use in evidence based decision making	Can be used as a basis for evidence based decision making

Chapter 3

Exercise 3.3: the research question

1 = Too broad and not specific enough

2 = Too narrow, it can be answered in a single sentence

3 = Suitable as a research question as tools exist to measure attitudes; for example, a survey could be performed.

4 = Too broad as the past has not been defined; the past could mean days, years, etc.

5 = Too broad as the word vocabulary is not defined

6 = Suitable as a research question as an experiment could be performed

7 = Too vague as the research group has not been defined

Exercise 3.4: types of hypothesis

1 = A loose non-directional hypothesis

2 = A loose directional hypothesis

3 = A loose non-directional hypothesis

4 = A loose non-directional hypothesis

5 = A loose directional hypothesis

6 = A loose non-directional hypothesis

7 = A directional research hypothesis

8 = A null hypothesis

9 = A complex hypothesis

Exercise 3.5: sampling

Example 1:

Stratified random sampling was used. The sample met the study criteria in that every participant was under the age of 45 years. However, the gender distribution was not representative as there were 825 women compared to only 175 men which does not reflect normal society. The demographics of the population were not explicit and it is not clear if only one geographical area was sampled.

Example 2:

Systematic random sampling was used. The sample was representative in terms of gender but not representative in terms of age as the age groups under 25 and over 55 years were not included which assumes that these groups do not use soap. Again, the demographics were not discussed and localities were not varied.

Exercise 3.8: types of variables

1 Independent variable = Violence on TV; Dependent variable = Increase in criminal behaviour.
2 Independent variable = Low fat diet; Dependent variable = Weight.
3 Independent variable = Giving women flowers; Dependent variable = Kiss.
4 Independent variable = Improved education; Dependent variable = Increase in concordance.
5 Independent variable = Mobilize directly after surgery; Dependent variable = Less post-operative pain.
6 Independent variable = District nursing notes at home *and* the regular contributions of health care professionals; Dependent variable = More effectively coordinated service.
7 Independent variable = World cup rugby *and* women spending time shopping; Dependent variable = Sudden upsurge in the national expenditure.

Chapter 4

Exercise 4.1: significance

1 = Significant
2 = Not significant
3 = Not significant
4 = Not significant
5 = Significant
6 = Not significant

Exercise 4.2: mean, median and mode

The mean is 72 (total) divided by 14 = 5.28.
The mode is 3 as this number appears 4 times.

The median is 4.5. This is calculated by first putting the numbers in order i.e. 2, 3, 3, 3, 3, 4, 4, 5, 5, 7, 7, 8, 9, 9. There are 14 numbers altogether so the 2 centre numbers 5 and 4 are added together equalling 9 and this is divided by 2 = 4.5.

Exercise 4.3: levels of data

1 = Nominal data as there is no order, just different groups
2 = Interval or ratio depending upon whether you believe that it is possible to have zero depression
3 = Ratio as it is possible to have no pain
4 = Nominal as there is no order, just groups
5 = Ratio as money is measured in pence and 1 is twice as much as two and there is the possibility to have zero pence
6 = Interval as it is not possible to have zero intelligence
7 = Ordinal as there is an order, i.e. gold is higher than silver but not twice as much
8 = Ratio as measurement occurs in equal amounts and it is possible to weigh zero kilogrammes
9 = Interval as it is not possible to have no satisfaction at all but the measurements occur at the same intervals.

Exercise 4.4: find me

1E, 2K, 3G, 4B, 5J, 6C, 7D, 8I, 9H, 10A, 11F

Chapter 5

Exercise 5.5: focus groups

Advantages

- the researcher can gain data very quickly as participants are interviewed collectively
- collectivity may enhance the confidence of the group to talk
- relatively inexpensive
- can capture those with limited literacy skills
- the researcher can validate the data
- can produce deep, rich data

Disadvantages

- the group can be dominated by very vocal participants
- there can be power differentials

- not suitable for sensitive topics
- some people may be reluctant to participate
- people can change their views to fit those of others
- findings can not be generalized
- researcher needs very good communication skills
- it is easy for the group to become out of control
- there is a lot of data to analyse so analysis is very time-consuming
- ethical issues as the researcher cannot maintain confidentiality and anonymity.

Chapter 6

Exercise 6.6: the differences between thematic analysis and the constant comparative method

- In thematic analysis data analysis occurs after all of the data has been collected but in grounded theory data collection and analysis happen simultaneously.
- In thematic analysis the sample size is determined at the start of the study but in grounded theory sampling continues until data saturation occurs.
- In thematic analysis a literature review precedes the data collection and informs the methodology but when using the constant comparative method the literature review is used at the end of the study to validate the themes and theory that has emerged.

Chapter 7

Exercise 7.1: types of triangulation

Two types of triangulation have been used: analysis triangulation as a coefficient which is quantitative was used and thematic analysis which is qualitative was also used, and methods triangulation was used which incorporated combining surveys, observations and interviews.

Chapter 8

Exercise 8.4: the key elements of an ethical piece of research

1   It must adhere to the Research Governance Framework (Department of Health 2001, 2005).
2   It must have ethical approval from the appropriate bodies.

3   It must be good for society and do no harm
4   All risks and benefits should be evaluated
5   The participants human rights should be protected
6   The researcher must ensure that confidentiality is assured
7   The participants' anonymity must be protected
8   The principles of justice must be upheld
9   The participants must give informed consent
10   The participants must be made aware of their right to withdraw at any time without prejudice
11   The researcher must be suitably skilled to carry out the research
12   The results should be accurately and truthfully communicated

Chapter 9

Exercise 9.1: suitable and unsuitable research topics

1   Topic one would be unsuitable as the topic is too focused to facilitate a literature search; many articles about rainbows would be found and many articles about caring could be identified but linking the two does not identify any useful material.
2   Topic two would be suitable as it is focused but not too narrow.
3   Topic three is far too broad and would identify too many articles.
4   Topic four would be suitable as it is focused and realistic. Identifying the UK NHS prevents the search being too broad.
5   Topic five would be unsuitable as the concepts under investigation are not a realistic fit. The bio-psycho-social elements of repetitive strain injury are difficult to identify and measure, and linking these to music played by a particular pop star would be too subjective to obtain any reliable results so the topic would not be a useful one.

Chapter 10

Exercise 10.3: contributing arguments

1   The use of narratives has become more noticeable in healthcare literature.
2   Over 35 articles were published in the *Journal of Effective Healthcare*.
3   There has been a dramatic increase in the number of researchers using this method.

Index

DOING A LITERATURE REVIEW IN HEALTH AND SOCIAL CARE
A Practical Guide
Second Edition

Helen Aveyard

9780335238859 (Paperback)
2010

eBook also available

This bestselling book is a step-by-step guide to doing a literature review in health and social care. It is vital reading for all those undertaking their undergraduate or postgraduate dissertation or any research module which involves a literature review.

The new edition has been fully updated and provides a practical guide to the different types of literature that you may be encountered when undertaking a literature review.

Key features:

- Includes examples of commonly occurring real life scenarios encountered by students
- Provides advice on how to follow a clearly defined search strategy
- Details a wide range of critical appraisal tools that can be utilised

www.openup.co.uk

OPEN UNIVERSITY PRESS
McGraw - Hill Education

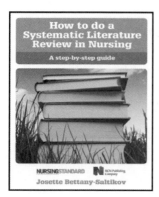

HOW TO DO A SYSTEMATIC LITERATURE REVIEW IN NURSING
A step-by-step guide

Josette Bettany-Saltikov

9780335242276 (Paperback)
January 2012

eBook also available

This is a step-by-step guide to doing a literature review in nursing that takes you through every step of the process from start to finish. From writing your review question to writing up your review, this practical book is the perfect workbook companion if you are doing your first literature review for study or clinical practice improvement.

The book features extracts from real literature reviews to help illustrate good practice as well as the pitfalls to avoid. Full of practical explanations this book will be invaluable at every stage. A must buy!

www.openup.co.uk

OPEN UNIVERSITY PRESS
McGraw - Hill Education